Lighthouse Early Church Fathers – St. Ambrose On the Death of His Brother

Lighthouse Early Church Fathers – St. Ambrose
On the Death of His Brother

Lighthouse Early Church Fathers – St. Ambrose
On the Death of His Brother

© Lighthouse Publishing 2018

All rights reserved. Without limiting the rights under copyright reserved above, no part of this publication may be reproduced, stored in a retrieval system, or transmitted, in any form or by any means (electronic, mechanical, photocopying, recording or otherwise), without the prior written permission of the copyright owner of this book.

Published by
Lighthouse Christian Publishing
SAN 257-4330
5531 Dufferin Drive
Savage, Minnesota, 55378
United States of America

www.lighthousechristianpublishing.com

TWO BOOKS OF ST. AMBROSE, BISHOP OF MILAN, ON THE DEATH OF HIS BROTHER SATYRUS

BOOK I.

1. WE have brought hither, dearest brethren, my sacrifice, a sacrifice undefiled, a sacrifice well pleasing to God, my lord and brother Satyrus. I did not forget that he was mortal, nor did my feelings deceive me, but grace abounded more exceedingly. And so I have nothing to complain of, but have cause for thankfulness to God, for I always desired that if any troubles should await either the Church or myself, they should rather fall on me and on my house. Thanks, therefore, be to God, that in this time of common fear, when everything is dreaded from the barbarian movements, I ended the trouble of all by my personal grief, and that I dreaded for all which was turned upon me. And may this be fully accomplished, so that my grief may be a ransom for the grief of all.

2. Nothing among things of earth, dearest brethren, was more precious to me, nothing more worthy of love, nothing more dear than such a brother, but public matters come before private. And should any one enquire what was his feeling; he would rather be slain for others than live for himself, because Christ died according to the flesh for all, that we might learn not to live for ourselves alone.

3. To this must be added that I cannot be ungrateful to God; for I must rather rejoice that I had such a brother than grieve that I had lost a brother, for the former is a gift, the latter a debt to be paid. And so, as long as I might, I enjoyed the loan entrusted to me, now He Who deposited the pledge has taken it back. There is no difference between denying that a pledge has been deposited and grieving at its being returned. In each there is untrustworthiness, and in each [eternal] life is risked. It is a fault if you refuse repayment, and piety if you refuse a sacrifice. Since, too, the lender of money can be made a fool of, but the Author of nature, the Lender of all that we need, cannot be cheated. And so the larger the amount of the loan, so much the more gratitude is due for the use of the capital.

4. Wherefore, I cannot be ungrateful concerning my brother, for he has given back that which was common to nature, and has gained what is peculiar to grace alone. For who would refuse the common lot? Who would grieve that a pledge specially entrusted to him is taken away, since the Father gave up His only Son to death for us? Who would think that he ought to be excepted from the lot of dying, who has not been excepted from the lot of being born? It is a great mystery of divine love, that not

even in Christ was exception made of the death of the body; and although He was the Lord of nature, He refused not the law of the flesh which He had taken upon Him. It is necessary for me to die, for Him it was not necessary. Could not He Who said of His servant, "If I will that he tarry thus until I come, what is that to thee?" not have remained as He was, if so He willed? But by continuance of my brother's life here, he would have destroyed his reward and my sacrifice. What is a greater consolation to us than that according to the flesh Christ also died? Or why should I weep too violently for my brother, knowing as I do that that divine love could not die.

5. Why should I alone weep more than others for him for whom you all weep? I have merged my personal grief in the grief of all, especially because my tears are of no use, whereas yours strengthen faith and bring consolation. You who are rich weep, and by weeping prove that riches gathered together are of no avail for safety, since death cannot be put off by a money payment, and the last day carries off alike the rich and the poor. You that are old weep, because in him you fear that you see the lot of your own children; and for this reason, since you cannot prolong the life of the body, train your children not to bodily enjoyment but to virtuous duties. And you that are young weep too, because the end of life is not the ripeness of old age. The poor too wept, and, which is of much more worth, and much more fruitful, washed away his transgressions with their tears. Those are redeeming tears, those are groanings which hide the grief of death, that grief which through the plenteousness of eternal joy covers over the feeling of former grief. And so, though the funeral be that of a private person, yet is the mourning

public; and therefore cannot the weeping last long which is hallowed by the affection of all.

6. For why should I weep for thee, my most loving brother, who was thus torn from me that thou might be the brother of all? For I have not lost but changed my intercourse with thee; before we were inseparable in the body, now we are undivided in affection; for thou remains with me, and ever wilt remain. And, indeed, whilst thou was living with me, our country never tore thee from me, nor didst thou thyself ever prefer our country to me; and now thou art become surety for that other country, for I begin to be no stranger there where the better portion of myself already is. I was never wholly engrossed in myself, but the greater part of each of us was in the other, yet we were each of us in Christ, in Whom is the whole sum of all, and the portion of each severally. This grave is more pleasing to me than thy natal soil, in which is the fruit not of nature but of grace, for in that body which now lies lifeless lies the better work of my life, since in this body, too, which I bear is the richer portion of thyself.

7. And would that, as memory and gratitude are devoted to thee, so, too, whatever time I have still to breathe this air, I could breathe it into thy life, and that half of my time might be struck off from me and be added to thine! For it had been just that for those, whose use of hereditary property was always undivided, the period of life should not have been divided, or at least that we, who always without difference shared everything in common during life, should not have a difference in our deaths.

8. But now, brother, whither shall I advance, or whither shall I turn? The ox seeks his fellow, and conceives itself incomplete, and by frequent lowing shows its tender longing, if perchance that one is wanting with whom it has been wont to draw the plough. And shall I, my brother, not long after thee? Or can I ever forget thee, with whom I always drew the plough of this life? In work I was inferior, but in love more closely bound; not so much fit through my strength, as endurable through thy patience, who with the care of anxious affection didst ever protect my side with thine, as a brother in thy love, as a father in thy care, as older in watchfulness, as younger in respect. So in the one degree of relationship thou didst expend on me the duties of many, so that I long after not one only but many lost in thee, in whom alone flattery was unknown, dutifulness was portrayed. For thou has nothing to which to add by pretence, inasmuch as all was comprised in thy dutifulness, so as neither to receive addition nor await a change.

9. But whither am I going, in my immoderate grief, forgetful of my duty, mindful of kindness received? The Apostle calls me back, and as it were puts a bit upon my sorrow, saying, as you heard just now: "We would not that ye should be ignorant, brethren, concerning them that sleep, that ye be not sorrowful, as the rest which have no hope." Pardon me, dearest brethren. For we are not
all able to say: "Be ye imitators of me, as I also am of Christ." But if you seek one to imitate, you have One Whom you may imitate. All are not fitted to teach, would that all were apt to learn.

10. But we have not incurred any grievous sin by our tears. Not all weeping proceeds from unbelief or weakness. Natural grief is one thing, distrustful sadness is another, and there is a very great difference between longing for what you have lost and lamenting that you have lost it. Not only grief has tears, joy also has tears of its own. Both piety excites weeping, and prayer waters the couch, and supplication, according to the prophet's saying, washes the bed. Their friends made a great mourning when the patriarchs were buried. Tears, then, are marks of devotion, not producers of grief. I confess, then, that I too wept, but the Lord also wept. He wept for one not related to Him, I for my brother. He wept for all in weeping for one, I will weep for thee in all, my brother.

11. He wept for what affected us, not Himself; for the Godhead sheds no tears; but He wept in that nature in which He was sad; He wept in that in which He was crucified, in that in which He died, in that in which He was buried. He wept in that which the prophet this day brought to our minds: "Mother Sion shall say, A man, yea, a man was made in her, and the Most High Himself established her." He wept in that nature in which He called Sion Mother, born in Judæa, conceived by the Virgin. But according to His Divine Nature He could not have a mother, for He is the Creator of His mother. So far as He was made, it was not by divine but by human generation, because He was made man, God was born.

12. But you read in another place: "Unto us a Child is born, unto us a Son is given." In the word Child is an indication of age, in that of Son the fullness of the Godhead. Made of His mother, born of the Father yet the Same Person was both born and given, you must not think

of two but of one. For one is the Son of God, both born of the Father and sprung from the Virgin, differing in order, but in name agreeing in one, as, too, the lesson just heard teaches for "a man was made in her and the Most High Himself established her;" man indeed in the body, the Most High in power. And though He be God and man in diversity of nature, yet is He at the same time one in each nature. One property, then, is peculiar to His own nature, another He has in common with us, but in both is He one, and in both is He perfect.

13. Therefore it is no subject of wonder that God made Him to be both Lord and Christ. He made Him Jesus, Him, that is, Who received the name in His bodily nature; He made Him of Whom also the patriarch David writes: "Mother Sion shall say, A man, yea, a man is made in her." But being made man He is unlike the Father, not in Godhead but in His body; not separated from the Father, but differing in office, abiding united in power, but separated in the mystery of the Passion.

14. The treatment of this topic demands more arguments, by which to demonstrate the authority of the Father, the special property of the Son, and the Unity of the whole Trinity; but to-day I have undertaken the office of consolation, not of discussion, although it is customary in consoling to draw away the mind from its grief by application to discussion. But I would rather moderate the grief than alter the affection, that the longing may rather be assuaged than lulled to sleep. For I have no wish to turn away too far from my brother, and to be led off by other thoughts, seeing that this discourse has been undertaken, as it were, for the sake of accompanying him,

that I might follow in affection him departing, and embrace in mind him whom I see with my eyes. For it gives me pleasure to fix the whole gaze of my eyes on him, to encompass him with kindly endearments; whilst my mind is stupefied, and I feel as though he were not lost whom I am able still to see present; and I think him not dead, my services to whom I do not as yet perceive to be wanting, services to which I had devoted the whole of my life and the drawing of every breath.

15. What, then, can I pay back in return for such kindness and such pains? I had made thee, my brother, my heir; thou hast left me as the heir; I hoped to leave thee as survivor, and thou hast left me. I, in return for thy kindnesses, that I might repay thy benefits, gave wishes; now I have lost my wishes yet not thy benefits. What shall I, succeeding to my own heir, do? What shall I do who outlive my own life? What shall I do, no longer sharing this light which yet shines on me? What thanks, what good offices, can I repay to thee? Thou hast nothing from me but tears. And perchance, secure of thy reward, thou desires not those tears which are all that I have left. For even when thou was yet alive, thou didst forbid me to weep, and didst show that our grief was more pain to thee than thine own death. Tears are bidden to flow no longer, and weeping is repressed. And gratitude to thee forbids them too, lest whilst we weep for our loss we seem to despair concerning thy merits.

16. But for myself at least thou lessens the bitterness of that grief; I have nothing to fear who used to fear for thee. I have nothing which the world can now snatch from me. Although our holy sister still survives, venerable for her

blameless life, thy equal in character, and not falling short in kindly offices; yet we both used to fear more for thee, we felt that all the sweetness of this life was stored up in thee. To live for thy sake was a delight, to die for thee were no cause of sorrow, for we both used to pray that thou might survive, it was no pleasure that we should survive thee. When did not our very soul shudder when a dread of this kind touched us? How were our minds dismayed by the tidings of thy sickness!

17. Alas for our wretched hopes! We thought that he was restored to us whom we see carried off, and we now recognize that thy departure hence was obtained by thy vows to the holy martyr Lawrence! And indeed I would that thou has obtained not only a safe passage hence, but also a longer time of life! Thou couldst have obtained many years of life, since thou was able to obtain thy departure hence. And I indeed thank Thee, Almighty Everlasting God, that Thou hast not denied us at least this last comfort, that Thou hast granted us the longed-for return of our much loved brother from the regions of Sicily and Africa; for he was snatched away so soon after his return as though his death were delayed for this alone, that he might return to his brethren.

18. Now, I clearly have my pledge which no change can any more tear from me; I have the relics which I may embrace, I have the tomb which I may cover with my body, I have the grave on which I may lie, and I shall believe that I am more acceptable to God, because I shall rest upon the bones of that holy body. Would that I had been able in like manner to place my body in the way of thy death! Has thou been attacked with the sword, I would have rather offered myself to be pierced for thee; had I

been able to recall thy life as it was passing away, I would have rather offered my own.

19. It profited me nothing to receive thy last breath, nor to have breathed into the mouth of thee dying, for I thought that either I myself should receive thy death, or should transfer my life to thee. O that sad, yet sweet pledge of the last kiss! O the misery of that embrace, in which the lifeless body began to stiffen, the last breath vanished! I tightened my arms indeed, but had already lost him whom I was holding; I drew in thy last breath with my mouth, that I might share thy death. But in some way that breath became life-giving to me, and even in death diffused an odor of greater love. And if I was unable to lengthen thy life by my breath, would that at least the strength of thy last breath might have been transfused into my mind, and that our affection might have inspired me with that purity and innocence of thine. Thou wouldst have left me, dearest brother, this inheritance, which would not smite the affections with tears of grief, but commend thine heir by notable grace.

20. What, then, shall I now do, since all the sweetness, all the solace, in fine, all the charms of that life are lost to me? For thou was alone my solace at home, my charm abroad; thou, I say, my adviser in counsel, the sharer in my cares, the averter of anxiety, the driver away of sorrow; thou was the protector of my acts and the defender of my thoughts; thou, lastly, the only one on whom rested care of home and of public matters. I call thy holy soul to witness that, in the building of the church, I often feared lest I might displease thee. Lastly, when thou came back thou didst chide thy delay. So was thou, at

home and abroad, the instructor and teacher of the priest, that thou didst not suffer him to think of domestic matters, and didst take thought to care for public matters. But I may not fear to seem to speak boastingly, for this is thy meed of praise, that thou, without displeasing any, both didst manage thy brother's house and recommend his priesthood.

21. I feel, indeed, that my mind is touched by the repetition of thy services and the enumeration of thy virtues, and yet in being thus affected I find my rest, and although these memories renew my grief, they nevertheless bring pleasure. Am I able either not to think of thee, or ever to think of thee without tears? And shall I ever be able either not to remember such a brother, or to remember him without tearful gratitude? For what has ever been pleasant to me that has not had its source in thee? What, I say, has ever been a pleasure to me without thee, or to thee without me? Had we not every practice in common, almost to our very eyesight and our sleep? Were our wills ever at variance? And what step did we not take in common? So that we almost seemed in raising our feet to move each other's body.

22. But if ever either had to go forth without the other, one would think that his side was unprotected, one could see his countenance troubled, one would suppose that his soul was sad, the accustomed grace, the usual vigor did not shine forth, the loneliness was a subject of dread to all, and made them fearful of some sickness. Such a strange thing it seemed to all that we were separated. I certainly, impatient at my brother's absence, and having it constantly in mind, kept on turning my head seeking him,

as it were, present, and seemed to myself then to see him and speak to him. But if I was disappointed in my hope, I seemed to myself, as it were, to be dragging a yoke on my bowed down neck, to advance with difficulty, to meet others with diffidence, and to return home hurriedly, since it gave me no pleasure to go farther without thee.

23. But when we both had to go forth, there were not more steps on the way than words, nor was our pace quicker than our talk, and it was less for the sake of walking than for the pleasure of conversing, for each of us hung on the lips of the other. We thought not of gazing intently on the view as we passed along, but listened to each other's anxious talk, drank in the kindly expression
of the eyes, and inhaled the delight of the brother's appearance. How I used silently to admire within myself thy virtues, how I congratulated myself that God had given me such a brother, so modest, so capable, so innocent, so simple, so that when I thought of thy innocence I began to doubt thy capability, when I saw thy capability I could hardly imagine thy innocence! But thou didst combine both with wonderful perfection.

24. Lastly, what we both had been unable to effect, thou didst accomplish alone. Prosper, as I hear, congratulated himself because he thought that on account of my priesthood he need not restore what he had purloined, but he found thy power alone to be greater than that of us both together. And so he paid all, and was not ungrateful for thy moderation, and did not scoff at thy modesty.
But for whom, brother, didst thou seek to gain that? We wished that should be the reward of thy labors which was the proof of them. Thou didst accomplish everything, and

when having done all thou didst return, thou alone, who art to be preferred to all, art torn from us; as if thou has put off death for this end, that thou might fulfil the office of affection, and then carry off the palm for capability.

25. How little, dearest brother, did the honors of this world delight us, because they separated us from one another! And we accepted them, not because the acquisition of them was to be desired, but that there might be no appearance of paltry dissimulation. Or perhaps they were therefore granted to us, that, inasmuch as by thy early death thou was about to shatter our pleasure, we might learn to live without each other.

26. And indeed I recognize the foreboding dread of my mind, when I often go again through what I have written. I endeavored to restrain thee, brother, from visiting Africa thyself, and wished thee rather to send some one. I was afraid to let thee go that journey, to trust thee to the waves, and a greater fear than usual came over my mind; but thou didst arrange the journey, and order the business, and, as I hear, didst entrust thyself again to the waves in an old and leaky vessel. For since thou was aiming at speed, thou didst set caution aside; eager to do me a kindness, thou made nothing of thy danger.

27. O deceitful joy! O the uncertain course of earthly affairs! We thought that he who was returned from Africa, restored from the sea, preserved after shipwreck, could not now be snatched from us; but, though on land, we suffered a more grievous shipwreck, for the death of him whom shipwreck at sea owing to strong swimming could not kill is shipwreck to us. For what enjoyment remains to

us, from whom so sweet an ornament has been taken, so bright a light in this world's darkness has been extinguished? For in him an ornament not only of our family but of the whole fatherland has perished.

28. I feel, indeed, the deepest gratitude to you, dearest brethren, holy people, that you esteem my grief as no other than your own, that you feel this bereavement as having happened to yourselves, that you offer me the tears of the whole city, of every age, and the good wishes of every rank, with unusual affection. For this is not the grief of private sympathy, but as it were a service and offering of public good-will. And should any sympathy with me because of the loss of such a brother touch you, I have abundant fruit from it, I have the pledge of your affection. I might prefer that my brother were living, but yet public kindness is in prosperity very pleasant, and in adversity very grateful.

29. And, indeed, so great kindness seems to me to merit no ordinary gratitude. For not without a purpose are the widows in the Acts of the Apostles described as weeping when Tabitha was dead, or the crowd in the Gospel, moved by the widow's tears and accompanying the funeral of the young man who was to be raised again. There is, then, no doubt that by your tears the protection of the apostles is obtained; no doubt, I say, that Christ is moved to mercy, seeing you weeping. Though He has not now touched the bier, yet He has received the spirit commended to Him, and if He have not called the dead by the bodily voice, yet He has by the authority of His divine power delivered my brother's soul from the pains of death and from the attacks of wicked spirits. And though he that

was dead has not sat up on the bier, yet he has found rest in Christ; and if he have not spoken to us, yet he sees those things which are above us, and rejoices in that he now sees higher things than we. For by the things which we read in the Gospels we understand what shall be, and what we see at present is a sign of what is to be.

30. He had no need of being raised again for time, for whom the raising again for eternity is waiting. For why should he fall back into this wretched and miserable state of corruption, and return to this mournful life, for whose rescue from such imminent evils and threatening dangers we ought rather to rejoice? For if no one mourns for Enoch, who was translated when the world was at peace and wars were not raging, but the people rather congratulated him, as Scripture says concerning him: "He was taken away, lest that wickedness should alter his understanding," with how much greater justice must this now be said, when to the dangers of the world is added the uncertainty of life. He was taken away that he might not fall into the hands of the barbarians; he was taken away that he might not see the ruin of the whole earth, the end of the world, the burial of his relatives, the death of fellow-citizens; lest, lastly, which is more bitter than any death, he should see the pollution of the holy virgins and widows.

31. So then, brother, I esteem thee happy both in the beauty of thy life and in the opportuneness of thy death. For thou was snatched away not from us but from dangers; thou didst not lose life but didst escape the fear of threatening troubles. For with the pity of thy holy mind for those near to thee, if thou knew that Italy was now

oppressed by the nearness of the enemy, how wouldst thou groan, how wouldst thou grieve that our safety wholly depended on the barrier of the Alps, and that the protection of purity consisted in barricades of trees! With what sorrow wouldst thou mourn that thy friends were separated from the enemy by so slight a division, from an enemy, too, both impure and cruel, who spares neither chastity nor life.

32. How, I say, couldst thou bear these things which we are compelled to endure, and perchance (which is more grievous) to behold virgins ravished, little children torn from the embrace of their parents and tossed on javelins, the bodies consecrated to God defiled, and even aged widows polluted? How, I say, couldst thou endure these things, who even with thy last breath, forgetful of thyself, yet not without thought for us, didst warn us concerning the invasion of the barbarians, saying that not in vain has thou said that we ought to flee. Perchance was it because thou didst see that we were left destitute by thy death, and thou didst it, not out of weakness of spirit, but from affection, and was weak with respect to us, but strong with respect to thyself. For when thou was summoned home by the noble man Symmachus thy parent, because Italy was said to be blazing with war, because thou was going into danger, because thou was likely to fall amongst enemies, thou didst answer that this was the cause of thy coming, that thou might not fail us in danger, that thou might show thyself a sharer in thy brother's peril.

33. Happy, then, was he in so opportune a death, because he has not been preserved for this sorrow. Certainly thou art happier than thy holy sister, deprived of thy comfort,

anxious for her own modesty, lately blessed with two brothers, now wretched because of both, being able neither to follow the one nor to leave the other; for whom thy tomb is a lodging, and the burying-place of thy body a home. And would that even this resting-place were safe! Our food is mingled with weeping and our drink with tears, for thou hast given us the bread of tears as food, and tears to drink in large measure, nay, even beyond measure.

34. What now shall I say of myself, who may not die lest I leave my sister, and desire not to live lest I be separated from thee? For what can ever be pleasant to me without thee, in whom was always my whole pleasure? or what satisfaction is it to remain longer in this life, and to linger on the earth where we lived with pleasure so long as we lived together? If there were anything which could delight us here, it could not delight without thee; and if ever we had earnestly desired to prolong our life, now at any rate we would not exist without thee.

35. This is indeed unendurable. For what can be endured without thee, such a companion of my life, such a sharer of my toil and partaker of my duties? And I could not even make his loss more endurable by dwelling on it beforehand, so much did my mind fear to think of any such thing concerning him! Not that I was ignorant of his condition, but a certain kind of prayers and vows had so clouded the sense of common frailty, that I knew not how to think anything concerning him except entire prosperity.

36. And then lately, when I was oppressed by a severe attack (would that it had been fatal), I grieved only that thou was not sitting by my couch, and sharing the kindly

duty with my holy sister might with thy fingers close my eyes when dead. What had I wished? What am I now pondering? What vows are wanting? What services are to succeed? I was preparing one thing, I am compelled to set forth another; not being the subject of the funeral rites but the minister. O hard eyes, which could behold my brother dying! O cruel and unkind hands, which closed those eyes in which I used to see so much! O still harder neck, which could bear so sad a burden, though it were in a service full of consolation.

37. Thou, my brother, has more justly done these things for me. I used to expect these services at thy hands, I used to long for them. But now, having survived my own life, what comfort can I find without thee, who alone use to comfort me when mourning, to excite my happiness and drive away my sorrow? How do I now behold thee, my brother, who now addresses no words to me, offers me no kiss? Though, indeed, our mutual love was so deeply seated in each of us, that it was cherished rather by inward affection than made public by open caresses, for we who professed such mutual trust and love did not seek the testimony of others. The strong spirit of our brotherhood had so infused itself into each of us, that there was no need to prove our love by caresses; but our minds being conscious of our affection, we, satisfied with our inward love, did not seem to require the show of caresses, whom the very appearance of each other fashioned for mutual love; for we seemed, I know not by what spiritual stamp or bodily likeness, to be the one in the other.

38. Who saw thee, and did not think that he had seen me? How often have I saluted those who, because they had

previously saluted thee, said that they had been already saluted by me? How many said something to thee, and related that they had said it to me? What pleasure, what amusement often was given me by this, because I saw that they were mistaken in us? What an agreeable mistake, what a pleasant slip, how innocent a deceit, how sweet a trick! For there was nothing for me to fear in thy words or acts, and I rejoiced when they were ascribed to me.

39. But if they insisted all too vehemently that they had given me some information, I used to smile and answer with delight: Take care that it was not my brother whom you told. For since we had everything in common, one spirit and one disposition, yet the secrets of friends alone were not common property, not that we were afraid of danger in the communication, but that we might keep
faith by withholding it. Yet if we had a matter to be consulted about, our counsel was always in common, though the secret was not always made common. For although our friends spoke to either of us, so that what they said might reach the other; yet I know that secrets were for the most part kept with such good faith that they were not imparted even to the other brother. For this is a convincing proof that was not betrayed without which had not been imparted to the brother.

40. I confess, then, that being raised by these so great and excellent benefits to a kind of mental ecstasy, I had ceased to fear that I might be the survivor, because I thought him more worthy to live, and therefore received the blow which I am unable to endure, for the wounds of such pain are more easily borne when dwelt upon beforehand than when unexpected. Who will now console

me full of sorrows? Who will raise up him that is smitten down? With whom shall I share my cares? Who will set me free from the business of this world? For thou was the manager of our affairs, the censor of the servants, the decider between brother and sister, the decider not in matters of strife but of affection.

41. For if at any time there was a discussion between me and my holy sister on any matter, as to which was the preferable opinion, we used to take thee as judge, who wouldst hurt no one, and anxious to satisfy each, didst keep to thy loving affection and the right measure in deciding, so as to let each depart satisfied, and gain for thyself the thanks of each. Or if thou thyself brought
anything for discussion, how pleasantly didst thou argue! and thy very indignation, how free from bitterness it was! how was thy discipline not unpleasant to the servants themselves! since thou didst strive rather to blame thyself before thy brethren than to punish through excitement! For our profession restrained in us the zeal for correction, and, indeed, thou, my brother, didst remove from us every inclination to correct, when thou didst promise to punish and desire to alleviate.

42. That is, then, evidence of no ordinary prudence, which virtue is thus defined by the wise. The first of good things is to know God, and with a pious mind to reverence Him as true and divine, and to delight in that loveable and desirable beauty of the eternal Truth with the whole affection of the mind. And the second consists in deriving from that divine and heavenly source of nature, love towards our neighbors, since even the wise of this world have borrowed from our laws. For they never could have

obtained those points for the discipline of men, except from that heavenly fount of the divine law.

43. What, then, shall I say of his reverence in regard to the worship of God? He, before being initiated in the more perfect mysteries, being in danger of shipwreck when the ship that bore him, dashed upon rocky shallows, was being broken up by the waves tossing it hither and thither, fearing not death but lest he should depart this life without the Mystery, asked of those whom he knew to be initiated the divine Sacrament of the faithful; not that he might gaze on secret things with curious eyes, but to obtain aid for his faith. For he caused it to be bound in a napkin, and the napkin round his neck, and so cast himself into the sea, not seeking a plank loosened from the framework of the ship, by floating on which he might be rescued, for he sought the means of faith alone. And so believing that he was sufficiently protected and defended by this, he sought no other aid.

44. One may consider his courage at the same time, for he, when the vessel was breaking up, did not as a shipwrecked man seize a plank, but as a brave man found in himself the support of his courage, nor did his hope fail nor his expectation deceive him. And then, when preserved from the waves and brought safe to land in the port, he first recognized his Leader, to Whom he had committed himself, and at once after either himself rescuing the servants, or seeing that they were rescued, disregarding his goods, and not longing for what was lost, he sought the Church of God, that he might return thanks for his deliverance, and acknowledge the eternal mysteries, declaring that there was no greater duty than

thanksgiving. But if not to be grateful to man has been judged like to murder, how enormous a crime is it not to be grateful to God!

45. Now it is the mark of a prudent man to know himself, and, as it has been defined by the wise, to live in accordance with nature. What, then, is so much in accordance with nature as to be grateful to the Creator? Behold this heaven, does it not render thanks to its Creator when He is seen? For "the heavens declare the glory of God, and the firmament proclaims His handy work." The sea itself when it is quiet and at rest sets forth a representation of the Divine Quiet; when it is stirred up, it shows that the wrath on high is terrible. Do we not all rightly admire the grace of God, when we observe that senseless nature restrains its waves as it were with sense and reason, and that the waves know their own limit? And what shall I say of the earth, which in obedience to the divine command freely supplies food to all living things; and the fields restore what they have received multiplied as it were by accumulating interest, and heaped up.

46. So he who by the guidance of nature had grasped the methods of the divine work in the ardent vigor of his mind, knew that thanks should be paid first of all to the Preserver of all; but inasmuch as he could not repay, he could at least feel grateful. For the essence of this thankfulness is that when it is offered it is felt, and by being felt is offered. So he offered thanks and brought away faith. For he who had felt such protection on the part of the heavenly Mystery wrapped in a napkin, how much did he expect if he received it with his mouth and drew it to the very depth of his bosom? How much more must he have been expecting of that, when received into

his breast, which had so benefited him when covered with a napkin?

47. But he was not so eager as to lay aside caution. He called the bishop to him, and esteeming that there can be no true thankfulness except it spring from true faith, he enquired whether he agreed with the Catholic bishops, that is, with the Roman Church? And possibly at that place the Church of the district was in schism. For at that time Lucifer had withdrawn from our communion, and although he had been an exile for the faith, and had left inheritors of his own faith, yet my brother did not think that there could be true faith in schism. For though schismatics kept the faith towards God, yet they kept it not towards the Church of God, certain of whose limbs they suffered as it were to be divided, and her members to be torn. For since Christ suffered for the Church, and the Church is the body of Christ, it does not seem that faith in Christ is shown by those by whom His Passion is made of none effect, and His body divided.

48. And so though he retained the deposit of faith, and feared to voyage as debtor of so vast an amount, yet he preferred to cross over to a place where he could make his payment in safety, for he was convinced that the payment of thankfulness to God consists in dispositions and faith, which payment, so soon as he had free access to the Church, he delayed not to make. And he both received the grace of God which he longed for, and preserved it when received. Nothing, then, can be wiser than that prudence which distinguishes between divine and human matters.

49. Why should I speak of his well-known eloquence in his forensic duties? What incredible admiration did he excite in the hall of justice of the high prefecture! But I prefer to speak of those things which he esteemed, through consideration of the mysteries of God, to be preferable to human matters.

50. And should any one wish more fully to regard his fortitude, let him consider how often after his shipwreck with invincible disregard of this life he crossed the sea and travelled through widespread regions in his journeys, and at last that at this very time he did not shrink from danger, but met it. Patient under injustice, regardless of cold, would that he had been equally thoughtful in taking precautions. But exactly herein was he blessed, that he, so long as his bodily strength allowed, spent his life fulfilling the work of youth, uninterruptedly carrying out what he wished to do, and paid no attention to his weakness.

51. But in what words can I set forth his simplicity? By this I mean a certain moderation of character and soberness of mind. Pardon me, I beseech you, and attribute it to my grief, if I allow myself to speak somewhat fully about him with whom I am no longer permitted to converse. And certainly it is an advantage for you to see that you have performed this kindly office not led by weak feelings, but by sound judgment; not as impelled by pity for his death, but moved by desire to do honor to his virtues; for every simple soul is blessed. And so great was his simplicity, that, converted as it were into a child, he was conspicuous for the simplicity belonging to that guileless age, for the likeness of perfect virtue, and for reflecting as in a mirror innocence of character.

Therefore he entered into the kingdom of heaven, because he believed the word of God, because he, like a child, rejected the artifices of flattery, and chose rather to accept with gentleness the pain of injustice than to avenge himself sharply; he was more ready to listen to complaints than to guile, ready for conciliation, inaccessible to ambition, holy in modesty, so that in him one would rather speak of excess of bashfulness than have to seek for such as is needful.

52. But the foundations of virtue are never in excess, for modesty does not hinder but rather commends the discharge of duty. And so was his face suffused with a certain virginal modesty, showing forth his inward feeling in his countenance, if perchance he had, coming on a sudden, met some female relative, he was as it were bowed down and sunk to the earth, though he was not different in company with men, he seldom lifted up his face, raised his eyes, or spoke; when he did one of these things, it was with a kind of bashful modesty of heart, with which, too, the chastity of his body agreed. For he preserved the gifts of holy baptism inviolate, being pure in body and still more pure in heart; fearing not less the shame of impurity in conversation than in his body; and thinking that no less regard was to be paid to modesty in purity of words than in chastity of body.

53. In fine, he so loved chastity as never to seek a wife, although in him it was not merely the desire of chastity, but also the grace of his love for us. But in a wonderful manner he concealed his feeling as to marriage, and avoided all boastfulness; and so carefully did he conceal

his feeling, that even when we pressed it on him, he appeared rather to postpone wedlock than to avoid it. So this was the one point with which he did not trust his brother and sister, not through any doubtful hesitation, but simply through virtuous modesty.

54. Who, then, could refrain from wondering that a man in age between a brother and a sister, the one a virgin, the other a priest, yet in greatness of soul not below either, should so excel in two great gifts, as to reflect the chastity of one vocation and the sanctity of the other, being bound not by profession but by the exercise of virtue. If, then, lust and anger bring forth other vices, I may rightly call chastity and gentleness as it were the parents of virtues; although, as it is the origin of all good things, so too is piety the seed-plot of other virtues.

55. What, then, shall I say of his economy, a kind of continence regarding possessions? For he who takes care of his own does not seek other men's goods, nor is he puffed up by abundance who is contented with his own. For he did not wish to recover anything except his own, and that rather that he might not be cheated than that he might be richer. For he rightly called those who seek other men's goods hawks of money. But if avarice be the root of all evils, he who does not seek for money has certainly stripped himself of vices.

56. Nor did he ever delight in more carefully prepared feasts or many dishes, except when he invited friends, wishing for what was sufficient for nature, not for superabundance for pleasure's sake. And, indeed, he was not poor in means, but was so in spirit. Certainly we ought

by no means to doubt of his happiness, who neither as a wealthy man delighted in riches, nor as a poor man thought that what he had was scanty.

57. It remains that, to come to the end of the cardinal virtues, we should notice in him the constituents of justice. For although virtues are related to each other and connected, still as it were a more distinct sketch of each is wanted, and especially of justice. For it being somewhat niggardly towards itself is wholly devoted to what is without, and whatever it has through a certain rigor
towards self, being carried away by love for all, it pours forth on its neighbors.

58. But there are many kinds of this virtue. One towards friends, another towards all men, another with respect to the worship of God or the relief of the poor. So what he was towards all, the affection of the people of the province over which he was set shows; who used to say that he was rather their parent than a judge, a kind umpire for loving clients, a steadfast awarder of just
law.

59. But what he was with his brother and sister, though all men were embraced in his good-will, our undivided patrimony testifies, and the inheritance neither distributed nor diminished, but preserved. For he said that love was no reason for making a will. This, too, he signified with his last words, when commending those whom he had loved, saying that it was his choice never to marry a wife, that he might not be separated from his brother and sister, and that he would not make a will, lest our feelings should in any point be hurt. Lastly, though begged and entreated

by us, he thought that nothing ought to be determined by himself, not, however, forgetting the poor, but only asking that so much should be given to them as should seem just to us.

60. By this alone he gave a sufficient proof of his fear of God, and set an example of religious feeling as regards men. For what he gave to the poor he offered to God, since "he that distributed to the poor lended unto God;" and by requiring what was just, he left them not a little, but the whole. For this is the total sum of justice, to sell what one has and give to the poor. For he who "hath dispersed, and hath given to the poor, his righteousness endures for ever." So he left us as stewards, not heirs; for the inheritance is to the heirs a matter of question, the stewardship is a duty to the poor.

61. So that one may rightly say that the Holy Spirit has this day told us by the voice of the boy reader: "He that is innocent in his hands and of a clean heart, who hath not lifted up his soul to vanity, nor used deceit unto his neighbor, this is the generation of them that seek the Lord." He, then, shall both ascend into the hill of the Lord and dwell in the tabernacle of God; because "he hath walked without spot, he hath worked righteousness, he hath spoken truth, he hath not deceived his neighbor;" nor did he lend his money for usury, who always wished [no more than] to retain that which was inherited.

62. Why should I relate that in his piety he went beyond mere justice, when he, having thought that in consideration of my office something ought to be given to the unlawful possessor of our property, declared that I

was the author of the bounty, but made over the receipts of his own share to the common fund.

63. These and other matters, which were then a pleasure to me, now sharpen the remembrance of my grief. They abide, however, and always will do so, nor do they ever pass away like a shadow; for the grace of virtue dies not with the body, nor do natural life and merits come to an end at the same time, although the use of natural life does not perish for ever, but rests in a kind of exemption for a time.

64. For one, then, who has performed such good deeds, and is rescued from perils, I shall weep rather from longing for him than for the loss. For the very opportuneness of his death bids us bear in mind that we must follow him rather with grateful veneration than grieve for him, for it is written that private grief should cease in public sorrow. This is said in the prophetical language, not only to that one woman, who is figured there, but to each, since it seems to be said to the Church.

65. To me, then, does this message come, and Holy Scripture says: "Dost thou teach this, is it thus that thou instructs the people of God? Knows thou not that thy example is a danger to others? save that perchance thou complains that thy prayer is not heard. First of all this is shameless arrogance, to desire to obtain for thyself what thou knows to have been denied to many, even saints, when thou art aware that God is no respecter of persons?" For although God is merciful, yet if He always heard all, He would appear to act no longer of His own free will,

but by a kind of necessity. Then, since all ask, if He were to hear all, no one would die. For how much dost thou daily pray? Is, then, God's appointment to be made void in consideration of thee? Why, then, dost thou lament that is sometimes not obtained, which thou knows cannot always be obtained?

66. "Thou fool," it says, "above all women, sees thou not our mourning, and what hath happened to us, how that Sion our mother is saddened with all sadness, and humbled with humbling. Mourn now also very sore, since we all mourn, and be sad since we all are sad, and thou art grieved for a brother. Ask the earth and she shall tell thee that it is she which ought to mourn, outliving so many that grow upon her. And out of her," it says, "were all born in the beginning, and out of her shall others come, and, behold, they walk almost all into destruction, and a multitude of them is utterly rooted out. Who, then, ought to make more mourning than she that hath lost so great a multitude, and not thou, which art sorry but for one?"

67. Let, then, the common mourning swallow up ours and cut off the bitterness of our private sorrow. For we ought not to grieve for those whom we see to be set free, and we bear in mind that so many holy souls are not without a purpose at this time loosed from the chains of the body. For we see, as if by God's decree, such reverend widows dying so closely at one time, that it seems to be a sort of setting out on a journey, not a sinking in death, lest their chastity in which they have served God their full time should be exposed to peril. What groans, what mourning, does so bitter a recollection stir up in me! And if I had no leisure for mourning, yet in my own personal grief, in the

loss of the very flower of so much merit, the common lot of nature consoled me; and my grief in consideration of one alone veiled the bitterness of the public funeral by the show of piety at home.

68. I seek again, then, O sacred Scripture, thy consolations, for it delights me to dwell on thy precepts and on thy sentences. How far more easy is it for heaven and earth to pass away, than for one tittle of the law to fail! But let us now listen to what is written: "Now," it says, "keep thy sorrow to thyself, and bear with a good courage the things which have befallen thee. For if thou shalt acknowledge the determination of God to be just, thou shalt both receive thy son in time, and shalt be praised among women." If this is said to a woman, how much more to a priest! If such words are said of a son it is certainly not unfitting that they should be uttered also concerning the loss of a brother; though if he had been my son I could never have loved him more. For as in the death of children, the lost labor and the pain borne to no purpose seem to increase the sorrow; so, too, in the case of brothers the habits of intercourse and joint occupations inflame the bitterness of grief.

69. But, lo! I hear the Scripture saying: "Do not continue this discourse, but allow thyself to be persuaded. For how great are the misfortunes of Sion! Be comforted in regard of the sorrow of Jerusalem. For thou sees that our holy places are polluted and the name that was called upon us is almost profaned, they that are ours have suffered shame, our priests are burnt, our Levites gone into captivity, our wives are polluted, our virgins suffer violence, our righteous men are carried away, our little

ones given up, our young men brought in bondage, and our strong men become weak. And, which is the greatest of all, the seal of Sion hast lost her glory, since now she is delivered into the hands of them that hate us. Do thou, then, shake off thy great heaviness, and put from thee the multitude of sorrows, that the Mighty may be merciful to thee again, and the Highest shall give thee rest by easing thy labors."

70. So, then, my tears shall cease, for one must yield to healthful remedies, since there ought to be some difference between believers and unbelievers. Let them, therefore, weep who cannot have the hope of the resurrection, of which not the sentence of God but the strictness of the faith deprives them. Let there be this difference between the servants of Christ and the worshippers of idols, that the latter weep for their friends, whom they suppose to have perished for ever; that they should never cease from tears, and gain no rest from sorrow, who think that the dead have no rest. But from us, for whom death is the end not of our nature but of this life only, since our nature itself is restored to a better state, let the advent of death wipe away all tears.

71. And certainly if they have ever found any consolation who have thought that death is the end of sensation and the failing of our nature, how much more must we find it so to whom the consciousness of good done brings the promise of better rewards! The heathen have their consolation, because they think that death is a cessation of all evils, and as they are without the fruit of life, so, too, they think that they have escaped all the feeling and pain of those severe and constant sufferings which we have to

endure in this life. We, however, as we are better supported by our rewards, so, too, ought we to be more patient through our consolation, for they seem to be not lost but sent before, whom death is not going to swallow up, but eternity to receive.

72. My tears shall therefore cease, or if they cannot cease, I will weep for thee, my brother, in the common sorrow, and will hide my private groaning in the public grief. For how can my tears wholly cease, since they break forth at every utterance of thy name, or when my very habitual actions arouse thy memory, or when my affection pictures thy likeness, or when recollection renews my grief. For how canst thou be absent who art again made present in so many occupations? Thou art present, I say, and art always brought before me, and with my whole mind and soul do I embrace thee, gaze upon thee, address thee, kiss thee; I grasp thee whether in the gloomy night or in the clear light, when thou vouch-safest to revisit and console me sorrowing. And now the very nights which used to seem irksome in thy lifetime, because they denied us the power of looking on each other; and sleep itself, lately, the odious interrupter of our converse, have commenced to be sweet, because they restore thee to me. They, then, are not wretched but blessed whose mutual presence fails not, whose care for each other is not lessened, whose mutual esteem is increased. For sleep is a likeness and image of death.

73. But if, in the quiet of night, our souls still cleaving to the chains of the body, and as it were bound within the prison bars of the limbs, yet are able to see higher and separate things, how much more do they see these, when

in their pure and heavenly senses they suffer from no hindrances of bodily weakness. And so when, as a certain evening was drawing on, I was complaining that thou didst not revisit me when at rest, thou was wholly present always. So that, as I lay with my limbs bathed in sleep, while I was [in mind] awake for thee, thou was alive to me, I could say, "What is death, my brother?" For certainly thou was not separated from me for a single moment, for thou was so present with me everywhere, that enjoyment of each other, which we were unable to have in the intercourse of this life, is now always and everywhere with us. For at that time certainly all things could not be present, for neither did our physical constitution allow it, nor could the sight of each other, nor the sweetness of our bodily embraces at all times and in all places be enjoyed. But the pictures in our souls were always present with us, even when we were not together, and these have not come to an end, but constantly come back to us, and the greater the longing the greater abundance have we of them.

74. So, then, I hold thee, my brother, and neither death nor time shall tear thee from me. Tears themselves are sweet, and weeping itself a pleasure, for by these the eagerness of the soul is assuaged, and affection being eased is quieted. For neither can I be without thee, nor ever forget thee, or think of thee without tears. O bitter days, which show that our union is broken! O nights worthy of tears, which have lost for me so good a sharer of my rest, so inseparable a companion! What sufferings would ye cause me, unless the likeness of him present offered itself to me, unless the visions of my soul

represented him whom my bodily sight shows me no more!

75. Now, now, O brother, dearest to my soul, although thou art gone by too early a death, happy at least art thou, who dost not endure these sorrows, and art not compelled to mourn the loss of a brother, separation from whom thou couldst not long endure, but didst quickly return and visit him again. But if then thou didst hasten to banish the weariness of my loneliness, to lighten the sadness of thy brother's mind, how much more often ought thou now to revisit my afflicted soul, and thyself lighten the sorrow which has its origin from thee!

76. But the exercise of my office now bids me rest awhile, and attention to my priestly duties draws my mind away; but what will happen to my holy sister, who though she moderates her affection by the fear of God, yet again kindles the grief itself of the affection by the zeal of her devotion? Prostrate on the ground, embracing her brother's tomb, wearied with toilsome walking, sad in spirit, day and night she renews her grief. For though she often breaks off her weeping by speech, she renews it in prayer; and although in her knowledge of her Scriptures she excels those who bring consolation, she makes up for her desire of weeping by the constancy of her prayers, renewing the abundance of her tears then chiefly, when no one can interrupt her. So thou hast that which thou mayest pity, not what thou mayest blame, for to weep in prayer is a sign of virtue. And although that be a common thing with virgins, whose softer sex and more tender affection abound in tears at the sight of the common weakness, even without the feeling of family grief, yet when there is

a greater cause for sorrowing, no limit is set to that sorrow.

77. The means of consolation, then, are wanting since excuses abound. For thou canst not forbid that which thou teaches, especially when she attributes her tears to devotion, not to sorrow, and conceals the course of the common grief for fear of shame. Console her, therefore, thou who canst approach her soul, and penetrate her mind. Let her perceive that thou art present, feel that thou art not departed, that having enjoyed his consolation of whose merit she is assured, she may learn not to grieve heavily for him, who warned her that he was not to be mourned for.

78. But why should I delay thee, brother, why should I wait that my address should die and as it were be buried with thee? Although the sight and form of thy lifeless body, and its remaining comeliness and figure abiding here, comfort the eyes, I delay no longer, let us go on to the tomb. But first, before the people I utter the last farewell, declare peace to thee, and pay the last kiss. Go before us to that home, common and waiting for all, and certainly now longed for by me beyond others. Prepare a common dwelling for him with whom thou hast dwelt, and as here we have had all things in common, so there, too, let us know no divided rights.

79. Do not, I pray thee, long put off him who is desirous of thee, expect him who is hastening after thee, help him who is hurrying, and if I seem to thee to delay too long, summon me. For we have not ever been long separated from each other, but thou was always wont to return. Nor

since thou canst not return again, I will go to thee; it is just that I should repay the kindness and take my turn. Never was there much difference in the condition of our life; whether health or sickness, it was common to both, so that if one sickened the other fell ill, and when one began to recover, the other, too, was convalescent. How have we lost our rights? This time, too, we had our sickness in common, how is it that death was not ours in common?

80. And now to Thee, Almighty God, I commend this guileless soul, to Thee I offer my sacrifice; accept favorably and mercifully the gift of a brother, the offering of a priest. I offer beforehand these first libations of myself. I come to Thee with this pledge, a pledge not of money but of life, cause me not to remain too long a debtor of such an amount. It is not the ordinary interest of a brother's love, nor the common course of nature, which is increased by such an amount of virtue. I can bear it, if I shall be soon compelled to pay it.

BOOK II.

ON THE BELIEF IN THE RESURRECTION.

1. IN the former book I indulged my longing to some extent, lest too sharp remedies applied to a burning wound might rather increase than assuage the pain. And as at the same time I often addressed my brother, and had him before my eyes, it was not out of place to let natural feelings have a little play, since they are somewhat satisfied by tears, soothed by weeping, and numbed by a shock. For the outward expression of affection is of a soft and tender nature, it loves nothing extravagant, nothing stern, nothing hard; and patience is proved by enduring rather than by resisting.

2. So, since the death-day might well, lately, by the sad spectacle draw aside the mind of a brother, because it occupied him wholly, now, inasmuch as on the seventh day, the symbol of the future rest, we return to the grave, it is profitable to turn our thoughts somewhat from my brother to a general exhortation addressed to all, and to give our attention to this; so as neither to cling to my brother with all our minds, lest our feelings overcome us, nor forgetting such devotion and desert, to turn wholly away from him; and in truth we should but increase the suffering of our intense grief, if his death were again the subject of to-day's address.

3. Wherefore we propose, dearest brethren, to console ourselves with the common course of nature, and not to think anything hard which awaits all. And therefore we deem that death is not to be mourned over; firstly, because it is common and due to all; next, because it frees

us from the miseries of this life and, lastly, because when in the likeness of sleep we are at rest from the toils of this world, a more lively vigor is shed upon us. What grief is there which the grace of the Resurrection does not console? What sorrow is not excluded by the belief that nothing perishes in death? nay, indeed, that by the hastening of death it comes to pass that much is preserved from perishing. So it will happen, dearest brethren, that in our general exhortation we shall turn our affections to my brother, and shall not seem to have wandered too far from him, if through hope of the Resurrection and the sweetness of future glory even in our discourse he should live again for us.

4. Let us then begin at this point, that we show that the departure of our loved ones should not be mourned by us. For what is more absurd than to deplore as though it were a special misfortune, what one knows is appointed unto all? This were to lift up the mind above the condition of men, not to accept the common law, to reject the fellowship of nature, to be puffed up in a fleshly mind, and not to recognize the measure of the flesh itself. What is more absurd than not to recognize what one is, to pretend to be what one is not? Or what can be a sign of less forethought than to be unable to bear, when it has happened, what one knew was going to happen? Nature herself calls us back, and draws us aside from sorrow of this sort by a kind of consolation of her own. For what so deep mourning is there, or so bitter grief, in which the mind is not at times relieved? For human nature has this peculiarity, that although men may be in sad circumstances, yet if only they be men, they sometimes turn their thoughts a little away from sadness.

5. It is said, indeed, that there have been certain tribes who mourned at the birth of human beings, and kept festival at their deaths, and this not without reason, for they thought that those who had entered upon this ocean of life should be mourned over, but that they who had escaped from the waves and storms of this world should be accompanied by rejoicing not without good reason. And we too forget the birthdays of the departed, and commemorate with festal solemnity the day on which they died.

6. Therefore, in accordance with nature, excessive grief must not be yielded to, lest we should seem either to claim for ourselves either an exceptional superiority of nature, or to reject the common lot. For death is alike to all, without difference for the poor, without exception for the rich. And so although through the sin of one alone, yet it passed upon all; that we may not refuse to acknowledge Him to be also the Author of death, Whom we do not refuse to acknowledge as the Author of our race; and that, as through one death is ours, so should be also the resurrection; and that we should not refuse the misery, that we may attain to the gift. For, as we read, Christ "is come to save that which was lost," and "to be Lord both of the dead and living." In Adam I fell, in Adam I was cast out of Paradise, in Adam I died; how shall the Lord call me back, except He find me in Adam; guilty as I was in him, so now justified in Christ. If, then, death be the debt of all, we must be able to endure the payment. But this topic must be reserved for later treatment.

7. It is now our purpose to demonstrate that death ought not to cause too heavy grief, because nature itself rejects

this. And so they say that there was a law among the Lycians, commanding that men who gave way to grief should be clothed in female apparel, inasmuch as they judged mourning to be soft and effeminate in a man. And it is inconsistent that those who ought to offer their breast to death for the faith, for religion, for their country, for righteous judgment, and the endeavor after virtue, should grieve too bitterly for that in the case of others which, if a fitting cause required, they would seek for themselves. For how can one help shrinking from that in ourselves which one mourns with too little patience when it has happened to others? Put aside your grief, if you can; if you cannot, keep it to yourself.

8. Is, then, all sorrow to be kept within or repressed? Why should not reason rather than time lighten one's sadness? Shall not wisdom better assuage that which the passage of time will obliterate? Further, it seems to me that it is a want of due feeling with regard to the memory of those whose loss we mourn, when we prefer to forget them rather than that our sorrow should be lessened by consolation; and to shrink from the recollection of them, rather than remember them with thankfulness; that we fear the calling to mind of those whose image in our hearts ought to be a delight; that we are rather distrustful than hopeful regarding the acceptance of the departed, and think of those we loved rather as liable to punishment than as heirs of immortality.

9. But you may say: We have lost those whom we used to love. Is not this the common lot of ourselves and the earth and elements, that we cannot keep for ever what has been

entrusted to us for a time? The earth groans under the plough, is lashed by rains, struck by tempests, bound by cold, burnt by the sun, that it may bring forth its yearly fruits; and when it has clothed itself with a variety of flowers, it is stripped and spoiled of its own adornment. How many plunderers it has! And it does not complain of the loss of its fruits, to which it gave birth that it might lose them, nor thereafter does it refuse to produce what it remembers will be taken from it.

10. The heavens themselves do not always shine with the globes of twinkling stars, wherewith as with coronets they are adorned. They are not always growing bright with the dawn of light, or ruddy with the rays of the sun; but in constant succession that most pleasing appearance of the world grows dark with the damp chill of night. What is more grateful than the light? what more pleasant than the sun? each of which daily comes to an end; yet we do not take it ill that these have passed away from us, because we expect them to return. Thou art taught in these things what patience thou ought to manifest with regard to those who belong to thee. If things above pass away from thee, and cause no grief, why should the passing away of man be mourned?

11. Let, then, grief be patient, let there be that moderation in adversity which is required in prosperity. If it be not seemly to rejoice immoderately, is it seemly so to mourn? For want of moderation in grief or fear of death is no small evil. How many has it driven to the halter, in how many hands has it placed the sword, that they might by that very means demonstrate their madness in not enduring death, and yet seeking it; in adopting that as a

remedy which they flee from as an evil. And because they were unable to endure and to suffer what is in agreement with their nature, they fall into that which is contrary to their desire, being separated for ever from those whom they desired to follow. But this is not common, since nature herself restrains although madness drives men on.

12. But it is common with women to make public wailing, as though they feared that their misery might not be known. They affect soiled clothing, as though the feeling of sorrow consisted therein; they moisten their unkempt hair with filth; and lastly, which is done habitually in many places, with their clothing torn and their dress rent in two, they prostitute their modesty in nakedness, as if they were ready to sacrifice that modesty because they have lost that which was its reward. And so wanton eyes are excited, and lust after those naked limbs, which were they not made bare they would not desire. Would that those filthy garments covered the mind rather than the bodily form. Lasciviousness of mind is often hidden under sad clothing, and the unseemly rudeness of dress is used as a covering to hide the secrets of wanton spirits.

13. She mourns for her husband with sufficient devotion who preserves her modesty and does not give up her constancy. The best duties to discharge to the departed are that they live in our memories and continue in our affection. She has not lost her husband who manifests her chastity, nor is she widowed as regards her union who has not changed her husband's name. Nor hast thou lost the heir when thou assists the joint-heir, but in exchange for a successor in perishable things thou hast a sharer in things eternal. Thou hast one to represent thine heir, pay to the

poor what was due to the heir, that there may remain one to survive, not only the old age of father or mother, but thine own life. Thou leaves thy successor all the more, if his share conduce not to luxury in things
present, but to the purchasing of things to come.

14. But we long for those whom we have lost. For two things specially pain us: either the longing for those we have lost, which I experience in my own case; or that we think them deprived of the sweetness of life, and snatched away from the fruits of their toil. For there is a tender movement of love, which suddenly kindles the affection, so as to have the effect rather of soothing than of hindering the pain; inasmuch as it seems a dutiful thing to long for what one has lost, and so under an appearance of virtue weakness increases.

15. But why dost thou think that she who has sent her beloved to foreign parts, and because of military service, or of undertaking some office, or has discovered that for the purpose of commerce he has crossed the sea, ought to be more patient than thou who art left, not because of some chance decision or desire of money, but by the law of nature? But, you say, the hope of regaining him is shut out. As though the return of any one were certain! And oftentimes doubt wearies the mind more where the fear of danger is strong; and it is more burdensome to fear lest something should happen than to bear what one already knows has happened. For the one increases the amount of fear, the other looks forward to the end of its grief.

16. But masters have the right to transfer their slaves whithersoever they determine. Has not God this right? It

is not granted to us to look for their return, but it is granted us to follow those gone before. And certainly the usual shortness of life seems neither to have deprived them of much who have gone before, nor to delay very long him who remains.

17. But if one cannot mitigate one's grief, does it not seem unbecoming to wish that because of our longing the whole course of things should be upset? The longings of lovers are certainly more intense, and yet they are tempered by regard to what is necessary; and though they grieve at being forsaken they are not wont to mourn, rather being deserted they blush at loving too hastily.
And so patience in regret is all the more manifested.

18. But what shall I say of those who think that the departed are deprived of the sweetness of life? There can be no real sweetness in the midst of the bitterness's and pains of this life, which are caused either by the infirmity of the body itself, or by the discomfort of things happening from without. For we are always anxious and in suspense as to our wishes for happier circumstances;
we waver in uncertainty, our hope setting before us doubtful things for certain, inconvenient for satisfactory, things that will fail for what is firm, and we have neither any strength in our will nor certainty in our wishes. But if anything happens against our wish, we think we are lost, and are rather broken down by pain at adversity than cheered by the enjoyment of prosperity. What good,
then, are they deprived of who are rather freed from troubles?

19. Good health, I doubt not, is more beneficial to us than bad health is hurtful. Riches bring more delights than poverty annoyance, the satisfaction in children's love is greater than the sorrow at their loss, and youth is more pleasant than old age is sad. How often is the attainment of one's wishes a weariness, and what one has longed for a regret; so that one grieves at having obtained what one was not afraid of obtaining. But what fatherland, what pleasures, can compensate for exile and the bitterness of other penalties? For even when we have these, the pleasure is weakened either by the disinclination to use or by the fear of losing them.

20. But suppose that some one remains unharmed, free from grief, in uninterrupted enjoyment of the pleasures of the whole course of man's life, what comfort can the soul attain to, enclosed in the bonds of a body of such a kind, and restrained by the narrow limits of the limbs? If our flesh shrinks from prison, if it abhors everything which denies it the power of roaming about; when it seems, indeed, to be always going forth, with its little powers of hearing or seeing what is beyond itself, how much more does our soul desire to escape from that prison-house of the body, which, being free with movement like the air, goes whither we know not, and comes whence we know not.

21. We know, however, that it survives the body, and that being set free from the bars of the body, it sees with clear gaze those things which before, dwelling in the body, it could not see. And we are able to judge of this by the instance of those who have visions of things absent and even heavenly in sleep (whose minds, when the body is as

it were buried in sleep, rise to higher things and relate them to the body). So, then, if death frees us from the miseries of this world, it is certainly no evil, inasmuch as it restores liberty and excludes suffering.

22. At this point the right place occurs for arguing that death is not an evil, because it is the refuge from all miseries and all evils, a safe harbor of security, and a haven of rest. For what adversity is there which we do not experience in this life? What storms and tempests do we not suffer? by what discomforts are we not harassed? whose merits are spared?

23. The holy patriarch Israel fled from his country, was exiled from his father, relatives, and home, he mourned over the shame of his daughter and the death of his son, he endured famine, when dead he lost his own grave, for he entreated that his bones should be translated, lest even in death he should find rest.

24. Holy Joseph experienced the hatred of his brethren, the guile of those who envied him, the service of slavery, the mastership of merchantmen, the wantonness of his mistress, the ignorance of her husband, and the misery of prison.

25. Holy David lost two sons; the one incestuous, the other a parricide. To have had them was a disgrace, to have lost them a grief. And he lost a third, the infant whom he loved. Him he wept for while still alive, but did not long for when dead. For so we read, that, while the child was sick, David entreated the Lord for him, and fasted and lay in sackcloth, and when the elders came

near to raise him from the earth, he would neither rise nor eat. But when he heard that the child was dead, he changed his clothes, worshipped God, and took food. When this seemed strange to his servants, he answered that he had rightly fasted and wept while the child was alive, because he justly thought that God might have mercy, and it could not be doubted that He could preserve the life of one alive Who could give life to the departed, but now, when death had taken place, why should he fast, for he could not now bring back him that was dead, and recall him who was lifeless. "I," said he, "shall go to him, but he shall not return to me."

26. O greatest consolation for him who mourns! O true judgment of a wise man! O wonderful wisdom of one who is a bond-man! that none should take it ill that anything adverse has happened to him, or complain that he is afflicted contrary to his deserts. For who art thou who beforehand proclaims thy deserts? Why desires thou to anticipate Him Who takes cognizance of all? Why does thou snatch away the verdict from Him Who is going to judge? This is permitted not even to the saints, nor has it ever been done by the saints with impunity. David confesses that he was scourged for this in his psalm: "Behold, these are the ungodly, who prosper in the world, they have obtained riches. Therefore I have cleansed my heart in vain, and washed my hands among the innocent; and I was scourged all the day long, and my accusation came every morning."

27. Peter also, though full of faith and devotion, yet because, not yet conscious of our common weakness, he had presumptuously said to the Lord, "I will lay down my

life for Thy sake," fell into the trial of his presumption before the cock crowed thrice. Although, indeed, that trial was a lesson for our salvation, that we might learn not to think little of the weakness of the flesh, lest through thus thinking little of it we should be tempted. If Peter was tempted, who can presume? who can maintain that he cannot be tempted? And without doubt for our sakes was Peter tempted, so that, the proving of the temptation did not take place in a stronger than he, but that in him we should learn how, resisting in temptations, although tried even by care for our lives, we might yet overcome the sting of the temptation with tears of patience.

28. But that same David, that the difference of his actions may not perhaps disturb those who cling to the words of Scripture; that same David, I say, who had not wept for the innocent infant, wept for the parricide when dead. For at the last, when he was wailing and mourning, he said, "O my son Absalom, my son Absalom! Who will grant me to die for thee!" But not only is Absalom the parricide wept over, Amnon is wept over; not only is the incestuous wept over, but is even avenged; the one by the scorn of the kingdom, the other by the exile of his brothers. The wicked is wept over, not the innocent. What is the cause? What is the reason? There is no little deliberation with the prudent and confirmation of results with the wise; for there is great consistency of prudence in so great a difference of actions, but the belief is one. He wept for those who were dead, but did not think that he ought to weep for the dead infant, for he thought that they were lost to him, but hoped that the latter would rise again.

29. But concerning the Resurrection more will be said later on; let us now return to our immediate subject. We have set forth that even holy men have without any consideration for their merits, suffered many and heavy things in this world, together with toil and misery. So David, entering into himself, says: "Remember; Lord, that we are dust; as for man, his days are but as grass;" and in another place: "Man is like to vanity, his days pass away as a shadow." For what is more wretched than we, who are sent into this life as it were plundered and naked, with frail bodies, deceitful hearts, weak minds, anxious in respect of cares, slothful as to labor, prone to pleasures.

30. Not to be born is then by far the best, according to Solomon's sentence. For they also who have seemed to themselves to excel most in philosophy have followed him. For he, before these philosophers in time, but later than many of our writers, spoke thus in Ecclesiastes: "And I praised all the departed, which are already dead, more than the living, who are yet alive. And better than both they is he who hath not yet been born, and who hath not seen this evil work which hath been done under the sun. And I saw all travail, and all the good of this labor, that for this a man is envied of his neighbor. And, indeed, this is vanity and vexation of spirit."

31. And who said this but he who asked for and obtained wisdom, to know how the world was made, and the power of the elements, the course of the year, and the dispositions of stars, to be acquainted with the natures of living creatures, the furies of wild beasts, and the violence of winds, and to understand the thoughts of man! How, then, should mortal matters be hidden from him, from whom heavenly things were not hidden? He who

penetrated the thoughts of the woman who was claiming the child of another, who by the inspiration of divine grace knew the natures of living creatures which he did not share; could he err or say what was untrue with regard to the circumstances of that nature, which he found in his own personal experience?

32. But Solomon was not the only person who felt this, though he alone gave expression to it. He had read the words of holy Job: "Let the day perish wherein I was born." Job had recognized that to be born is the beginning of all woes, and therefore wished that the day on which he was born might perish, so that the origin of all troubles might be removed, and wished that the day of his birth might perish that he might receive the day of resurrection. For Solomon had heard his father's saying: "Lord, make me to know mine end, and the number of my days, that I may know what is lacking unto me." For David knew that what is perfect cannot be grasped here, and therefore hastened on to those things which are to come. For now we know in part, and understand in part, but then it will be possible for that which is perfect to be grasped, when not the shadow but the reality of the Divine Majesty and eternity shall begin to shine so as to be gazed upon by us with unveiled face.

33. But no one would hasten to the end, except he were fleeing from the discomfort of this life. And so David also explained why he hastened to the end, when he said: "Behold Thou hast made my days old, and my being is as nothing before Thee, surely all things are vanity, even every man that lives." Why, then, do we hesitate to flee from vanity? Or why does it please us to be troubled to no

purpose in this world, to lay up treasures, and not know for what heir we are gathering them? Let us pray that troubles be removed from us, that we be taken out of this foolish world, that we may be free from our daily pilgrimage, and return to that country and our natural home. For on this earth we are strangers and foreigners; we have to return thither whence we have come down, we must strive and pray not perfunctorily but earnestly to be delivered from the guile and wickedness of men full of words. And he who knew the remedy groaned that his sojourn was prolonged, and that he must dwell with the unjust and sinners. What shall I do, who both am sinful and know not the remedy?

34. Jeremiah also bewails his birth in these words: "Woe is me, my mother! Why hast thou borne me a man of contention in all the earth? I have not benefited others, nor has any one benefited me, my strength hath failed." If, then, holy men shrink from life whose life, though profitable to us, is esteemed unprofitable to themselves; what ought we to do who am not able to profit others, and who feel that it, like money borrowed at interest, grows more heavily weighted every day with an increasing mass of sins?

35. "I die daily," says the Apostle. Better certainly is this saying than theirs who said that meditation on death was true philosophy, for they praised the study, he exercised the practice of death. And they acted for themselves only, but Paul, himself perfect, died not for his own weakness but for ours. But what is meditation on death but a kind of separation of body and soul, for death itself is defined as

nothing else than the separation of body and soul? But this is in accordance with common opinion.

36. But according to the Scriptures we have been taught that death is threefold. One death is when we die to sin, but live to God. Blessed, then, is that death which, escaping from sin, and devoted to God, separates us from what is mortal and consecrates us to Him Who is immortal. Another death is the departure from this life, as the patriarch Abraham died, and the patriarch David, and were buried with their fathers; when the soul is set free from the bonds of the body. The third death is that of which it is said: "Leave the dead to bury their own dead." In that death not only the flesh but also the soul dies, for "the soul that sinned, it shall die." For it dies to the Lord, through the weakness not of nature but of guilt. But this death is not the discharge from this life, but a fall through error.

37. Spiritual death, then, is one thing, natural death another, a third the death of punishment. But that which is natural is not also penal, for the Lord did not inflict death as a penalty, but as a remedy. And to Adam when he sinned, one thing was appointed as a penalty, another for a remedy, when it was said: "Because thou hast hearkened unto the voice of thy wife, and hast eaten of the tree of which I had commanded thee that of it alone thou should not eat, cursed is the ground in thy labor; in sorrow shalt thou eat its fruit all the days of thy life. Thorns and thistles shall it bring forth to thee, and thou shalt eat the herb of the field. In the sweat of thy face shalt thou eat thy bread, till thou return to the earth from which thou was taken."

38. Here you have the days of rest from penalties, for they contain the punishment decreed against the thorns of this life, the cares of the world, and the pleasures of riches which shut out the Word. Death is given for a remedy, because it is the end of evils. For God said not, "Because thou hast hearkened to the voice of the woman thou shalt return to the earth," for this would have been a penal sentence, as this one is, "The earth under curse shall bring forth thorns and thistles to thee;" but He said: "In sweat shalt thou eat thy bread until thou return to the earth." You see that death is rather the goal of our penalties, by which an end is put to the course of this life.

39. So, then, death is not only not an evil, but is even a good thing. So that it is sought as a good, as it is written: "Men shall seek death and shall not find it." They will seek it who shall say to the mountains: "Fall on us, and to the hills, Cover us." That soul, too, shall seek it which has sinned. That rich man lying in hell shall seek it, who wishes that his tongue should be cooled with the finger of Lazarus.

40. We see, then, that this death is a gain and life a penalty, so that Paul says: "To me to live is Christ and to die is gain." What is Christ but the death of the body, the breath of life? And so let us die with Him, that we may live with Him. Let there then be in us as it were a daily practice and inclination to dying, that by this separation from bodily desires, of which we have spoken, our soul may learn to withdraw itself, and, as it were placed on high, when earthly lusts cannot approach and attach it to themselves, may take upon herself the likeness of death, that she incur not the penalty of death. For the law of the

flesh wars against the law of the mind, and makes it over to the law of error, as the Apostle has made known to us, saying: "For I see a law of the flesh in my members warring against the law of my mind, and bringing me into captivity in the law of sin." We are all attached, we all feel this; but we are not all delivered. And so a miserable man am I, unless I seek the remedy.

41. But what remedy? "Who shall deliver me out of the body of this death? Thanks be to God through Jesus Christ our Lord." We have a physician, let us use the remedy. Our remedy is the grace of Christ, and the body of death is our body. Let us therefore be as strangers to our body, lest we be strangers to Christ. Though we are in the body, let us not follow the things which are of the body, let us not reject the rightful claims of nature, but desire before all the gifts of grace: "For to be dissolved and to be with Christ is far better; yet to abide in the flesh is more needful for your sakes."

42. But this need is not the case of all, Lord Jesus; it is not so with me, who am profitable to none; for to me death is a gain, that I may sin no more. To die is gain to me, who, in the very treatise in which I comfort others, am incited as it were by an intense impulse to the longing for my lost brother, since it suffers me not to forget him. Now I love him more, and long for him more intensely. I long for him when I speak, I long for him when I read again what I have written, and I think that I am more impelled to write this, that I may not ever be without the recollection of him. And in this I am not acting contrary to Scripture, but I am of the same mind with Scripture, that I may grieve with more patience, and long with greater intensity.

43. Thou hast caused me, my brother, not to fear death, and I only would that my life might die with thine! This Balaam wished for as the greatest good for himself, when, inspired by the spirit of prophecy, he said: "Let my soul die in the souls of the righteous, and let my seed be like the seed of them." And in truth he wished this according to the spirit of prophecy, for as he saw the rising of Christ, so also he saw His triumph, he saw His death, but saw also in Him the everlasting resurrection of men, and therefore feared not to die as he was to rise again. Let not then my soul die in sin, nor admit sin into itself, but let it die in the soul of the righteous, that it may receive his righteousness. Then, too, he who dies in Christ is made a partaker of His grace in the Font.

44. Death is not, then, an object of dread, nor bitter to those in need, nor too bitter to the rich, nor unkind to the old, nor a mark of cowardice to the brave, nor everlasting to the faithful nor unexpected to the wise. For how many have consecrated their life by the renown of their death alone, how many have been ashamed to live, and have found death a gain! We have read how often by the death of one great nations have been delivered; the armies of the enemy have been put to flight by the death of the general, who had been unable to conquer them when alive.

45. By the death of martyrs religion has been defended, faith increased, the Church strengthened; the dead have conquered, the persecutors have been overcome. And so we celebrate the death of those of whose lives we are ignorant. So, too, David rejoiced in prophecy at the departure of his own soul, saying: "Precious in the sight

of the Lord is the death of His saints." He esteemed death better than life. The death itself of the martyrs is the prize of their life. And again, by the death of those at variance hatred is put an end to.

46. Why should more be said? By the death of One the world was redeemed. For Christ, had He willed, need not have died, but He neither thought that death should be shunned as though there were any cowardice in it, nor could He have saved us better than by dying. And so His death is the life of all. We are signed with the sign of His death, we show forth His death when we pray; when we offer the Sacrifice we declare His death, for His death is victory, His death is our mystery, His death is the yearly recurring solemnity of the world. What now should we say concerning His death, since we prove by this Divine Example that death alone found immortality, and that death itself redeemed itself. Death, then, is not to be mourned over, for it is the cause of salvation for all; death is not to be shunned, for the Son of God did not think it unworthy of Him, and did not shun it. The order of nature is not to be loosed, for what is common to all cannot admit of exception in individuals.

47. And, indeed, death was no part of man's nature, but became natural; for God did not institute death at first, but gave it as a remedy. Let us then take heed that it do not seem to be the opposite. For if death is a good, why is it written that "God made not death, but by the malice of men death entered into the world"? For of a truth death was no necessary part of the divine operation, since for those who were placed in paradise a continual succession of all good things streamed forth; but because of

transgression the life of man, condemned to lengthened labor, began to be wretched with intolerable groaning; so that it was fitting that an end should be set to the evils, and that death should restore what life had lost. For immortality, unless grace breathed upon it, would be rather a burden than an advantage.

48. And if one consider accurately, it is not the death of our being, but of evil, for being continues, it is evil that perishes. That which has been rises again; would that as it is now free from sinning, so it were without former guilt! But this very thing is a proof that it is not the death of being, that we shall be the same persons as we were. And so we shall either pay the penalty of our sins, or attain to the reward of our good deeds. For the same being will rise again, now more honorable for having paid the tax of death. And then "the dead who are in Christ shall rise first; then, too, we who are alive," it is said, "shall together with them be caught up in the clouds into the air to meet the Lord, and so we shall always be with the Lord." They first, but those that are alive second. They with Jesus, those that are alive through Jesus. To them life will be sweeter after rest, and though the living will have a delightful gain, yet they will be without experience of the remedy.

49. There is, then, nothing for us to fear in death, nothing for us to mourn, whether life which was received from nature be rendered up to her again, or whether it be sacrificed to some duty which claims it, and this will be either an act of religion or the exercise of some virtue. And no one ever wished to remain as at present. This has been supposed to have been promised to John, but it is not

the truth. We hold fast to the words, and deduce the meaning from them. He himself in his own writing denies that there was a promise that he should not die, that no one from that instance might yield to an empty hope. But if to wish for this would be an extravagant hope, how much more extravagant were it to grieve without rule for what has happened according to rule!

50. The heathen mostly console themselves with the thought, either of the common misery, or of the law of nature, or of the immortality of the soul. And would that their utterances were consistent, and that they did not transmit the wretched soul into a number of ludicrous monstrosities and figures! But what ought we to do, whose reward is the resurrection, though many, not being able to deny the greatness of this gift, refuse to believe in it? And for this reason will we maintain it, not by one casual argument only, but by as many as we are able.

51. All things, indeed, are believed to be, either because of experience, or on grounds of reason, or from similar instances, or because it is fitting that they be, and each of these supports our belief. Experience teaches us that we are moved; reason, that which moves us must be considered the property of another power; similar instances show that the field has borne crops, and therefore we expect that it will continue to bear them. Fitness, because even where we do not think that there will be results, yet we believe that it is by no means fitting to give up the works of virtue.

52. Each, then, is supported by each. But belief in the resurrection is inferred most clearly on three grounds, in

which all are included. These are reason, analogy from universal example, and the evidence of what has happened, since many have risen. Reason is clear. For since the whole course of our life consists in the union of body and soul, and the resurrection brings with it either the reward of good works, or the punishment of wicked ones, it is necessary that the body, whose actions are weighed, rise again. For how shall the soul be summoned to judgment without the body, when account has to be rendered of the companionship of itself and the body?

53. Rising again is the lot of all, but there is a difficulty in believing this, because it is not due to our deserts, but is the gift of God. The first argument for the resurrection is the course of the world, and the condition of all things, the series of generations, the changes in the way of succession, the setting and rising of constellations, the ending of day and night, and their daily succession coming as it were again to life. And no other reason can exist for the fertile temperament of this earth, but that the divine order restores by the dews of night as much of that moisture from which all earthly things are produced, as the heat of the sun dries up by day. Why should I speak of the fruits of the earth? Do they not seem to die when they fall, to rise again when they grow green once more? That which is sown rises again, that which is dead rises again, and they are formed once more into the same classes and kinds as before. The earth first gave back these fruits, in these first our nature found the pattern of the resurrection.

54. Why doubt that body shall rise again from body? Grain is sown, grain comes up again: fruit is sown, fruit comes up again; but the grain is clothed with blossom and

husk. "And this mortal must put on immortality, and this corruptible must put on incorruption." The blossom of the resurrection is immortality, the blossom of the resurrection is incorruption. For what is more fruitful than perpetual rest? what supplied with richer store than everlasting security? Here is that abundant fruit, by whose increase man's nature shoots forth more abundantly after death.

55. But you wonder how what has yielded to putrefaction can again become solid, how scattered particles can come together, those that are consumed be made good: you do not wonder how seeds broken up under the moist pressure of the earth grow green. For certainly they too, rotting under contact with the earth, are broken up, and when the fertilizing moisture of the soil gives life to the dead and hidden seeds, and, by the vital warmth, as it were breathing out a kind of soul of the green herb. Then by little and little nature raises from the ground the tender stalk of the growing ear, and as a careful mother folds it in certain sheaths, lest the sharp ice should hurt it as it grows, and to protect it from too great heat of the sun; and lest after this the rain should break down the fruit itself escaping as it were from its first cradle and just grown up, or lest the wind should scatter it, or small birds destroy it, she usually hedges it around with a fence of bristling awn.

56. Why should one, then, be surprised if the earth give back those bodies of men which it has received, seeing that it gives life to, raises, clothes, protects, and defends whatsoever bodies of seeds it has received? Cease then to doubt that the trustworthy earth, which restores multiplied as it were by usury the seeds committed to it, will also

restore the entrusted deposit of the race of man. And why should I speak of the kinds of trees, which spring up from seed sown, and with revivified fruitfulness bear again their opening fruits, and repeat the old shape and likeness, and certain trees being renewed continue through many generations, and in their endurance overpass the very centuries? We see the grape rot, and the vine come up again: a graft is inserted and the tree is born again. Is there this divine foresight for restoring trees, and no care for men? And He Who has not suffered to perish that which He gave for man's use, shall He suffer man to perish, whom he made after His own image?

57. But it appears incredible to you that the dead rise again? "Thou foolish one, that which thou thyself sows, does it not first die that it may be quickened?" Sow any dry seed you please, it is raised up. But, you answer, it has the life-juice in itself. And our body has its blood, has its own moisture. This is the life-juice of our body. So that I think that the objection is exploded which some allege that a dry twig does not revive, and then endeavor to argue from this to the prejudice of the flesh. For the flesh is not dry, since all flesh is of clay, clay comes from moisture—moisture from the earth. Then, again, many growing plants, though always fresh, spring from dry and sandy soil, since the earth itself supplies sufficient moisture for itself. Does the earth then, which continually restores all things, fail with regard to man? From what has been said it is clear that we must not doubt that it is rather in accordance with than contrary to nature; for it is natural that all things living should rise again, but contrary to nature that they should perish.

58. We come now to a point which much troubles the heathen, how it can be that the earth should restore those whom the sea has swallowed up, wild beasts have torn to pieces or have devoured. So, then, at last we necessarily come to the conclusion that the doubt is not as to belief in resurrection in general, but as to a part. For, granted that the bodies of those torn in pieces do not rise again, the others do so, and the resurrection is not disproved, but a certain class is an exception. Yet I wonder why they think there is any doubt even concerning these, as though not all things which are of the earth return to the earth, and crumble again into earth. And the sea itself for the most part casts up on neighboring shores whatever human bodies it has swallowed. And if this were not so, I suppose we are to believe that it would not be difficult for God to join together what was dispersed, to unite what was scattered; God, Whom the universe obeys, to Whom the dumb elements submit and nature serves; as though it were not a greater wonder to give life to clay than to join it together.

59. That bird in the country of Arabia, which is called the Phoenix, restored by the renovating juices of its flesh, after being dead comes to life again: shall we believe that men alone are not raised up again? Yet we know this by common report and the authority of writings, namely, that the bird referred to has a fixed period of life of five hundred years, and when by some warning of nature it knows that the end of its life is at hand, it furnishes for itself a casket of frankincense and myrrh and other perfumes, and its work and the time being together ended, it enters the casket and dies. Then from its juices a worm comes forth, and grows by degrees into the fashion of the

same bird, and its former habits are restored, and borne up by the oarage of its wings it commences once more the course of its renewed life, and discharges a debt of gratitude. For it conveys that casket, whether the tomb of its body or the cradle of its resurrection, in which quitting life it died, and dying it rose again, from Ethiopia to Lycaonia; and so by the resurrection of this bird the people of those regions understand that a period of five hundred years is accomplished. So to that bird the five hundredth is the year of resurrection, but to us the thousandth: it has its resurrection in this world, we have ours at the end of the world. Many think also that this bird kindles its own funeral pile, and comes to life again from its own ashes.

60. But perhaps nature if more deeply investigated will seem to give a deeper reason for our belief: let our thoughts turn back to the origin and commencement of the creation of man. You are men and women, you are not ignorant of the things which have to do with human nature, and if any of you have not this knowledge, you know that we are born of nothing. But how small an origin for being so great as we are! And if I do not speak more plainly, yet you understand what I mean, or rather what I will not say. Whence, then, is this head, and that wonderful countenance, whose maker we see not? We see the work, it is fashioned for various purposes and uses. Whence is this upright figure, this lofty stature, this power of action, this quickness of perception, this capacity for walking upright? Doubtless the organs of nature are not known to us, but that which they effect is known. Thou too was once seed, and thy body is the seed of that which shall rise again. Listen to Paul and learn that thou art this

seed: "It is sown in corruption, it shall rise in incorruption; it is sown in dishonor, it shall rise in glory; it is sown in weakness, it shall rise in power; it is sown a natural body, it shall rise a spiritual body." Thou also, then, art sown as are other things, why wonders thou if thou shalt rise again as shall others? But thou believes as to them, because thou sees; thou believes not this, because thou sees it not: "Blessed are they that have not seen, and yet have believed."

61. However, before the season comes, those things also are not believed, for every season is not suited for the raising of seeds. Wheat is sown at one time, and comes up at another; at one time the vine is planted, at another the budding twigs begin to shoot, the foliage grows luxuriant, and the grape is formed; at one time the olive is planted, at another time, as though pregnant and loaded with its offspring of berries, it is bent down by the abundance of its fruit. But before its own period arrives for each, the produce is restricted, and that which bears has not the age of bearing in its own power. One may see the mother of all at one time disfigured with mould, at another bare of produce, at another green and full of flowers, at another dried up. Any spot which might wish to be always clothed and never to lay aside the golden dress of its seeds, or the green dress of the meadows, would be barren in itself and unendowed with the gain of its own produce which it would have transferred to others.

62. So, then, even if thou wilt not believe in our resurrection by faith nor by example, thou wilt believe by experience. For many products, as the vine, the olive, and different fruits, the end of the year is the fit time for

ripening; and for us also the consummation of the world, as though the end of the year has set the fitting time for rising again. And fitly is the resurrection of the dead at the consummation of the world, lest after the resurrection we should have to fall back into this evil age. For this cause Christ suffered that He might deliver us from this evil world; lest the temptations of this world should overthrow us again, and it should be an injury to us to come again to life, if we came to life again for sin.

63. So then we have both a reason and a time for the resurrection: a reason because nature in all its produce remains consistent with itself, and does not fail in the generation of men alone; a time because all things are produced at the end of the year. For the seasons of the world consist of one year. What wonder if the year be one since the day is one. For on one day the Lord hired the laborers to work in the vineyard, when He said, "Why stand ye here all the day idle?"

64. The causes of the beginnings of all things are seeds. And the Apostle of the Gentiles has said that the human body is a seed. And so in succession after sowing there is the substance needful for the resurrection. But even if there were no substance and no cause, who could think it difficult for God to create man anew whence He will and as He wills. Who commanded the world to come into being out of no matter and no substance? Look at the heaven, behold the earth. Whence are the fires of the stars? Whence the orb and rays of the sun? Whence the globe of the moon? Whence the mountain heights, the hard rocks, the woody groves? Whence are the air diffused around, and the waters, whether enclosed or poured abroad? But if God made all these things out of

nothing (for "He spoke and they were made, He commanded and they were created"), why should we wonder that which has been should be brought to life again, since we see produced that which had not been?

65. It is a cause for wonder that though they do not believe in the resurrection, yet in their kindly care they make provision that the human race should not perish, and so say that souls pass and migrate into other bodies that the world may not pass away. But let them say which is the most difficult, for souls to migrate, or to return; come back to that which is their own, or seek for fresh dwelling places.

66. But let those who have not been taught doubt. For us who have read the Law, the Prophets, the Apostles, and the Gospel it is not lawful to doubt. For who can doubt when he reads: "And in that time shall all thy people be saved which is written in the book; and many of them that sleep in the graves of the earth shall arise with one opening, these to everlasting life, and those to shame and everlasting confusion. And they that have understanding shall shine as the brightness of the firmament, and of the just many shall be as the stars for ever." Well, then, did he speak of the rest of those that sleep, that one may understand that death lasts not for ever, which like sleep is undergone for a time, and is put off at its time; and he shows that the progress of that life which shall be after death is better than that which is passed in sorrow and pain before death, inasmuch as the former is compared to the stars, the latter is assigned to trouble.

67. And why should I bring together what is written elsewhere: "Thou shalt raise me up and I will praise Thee." Or that other passage in which holy Job, after experiencing the miseries of this life, and overcoming all adversity by his virtuous patience, promised himself a recompense for present evils in the resurrection, saying: "Thou shalt raise up this body of mine which has suffered many evils." Isaiah also, proclaiming the resurrection to the people, says that he is the announcer of the Lord's message, for we read thus: "For the mouth of the Lord hath spoken, and they shall say in that day." And what the mouth of the Lord declared that the people should say is set forth later on, where it is written: "Because of Thy fear, O Lord, we have been with child and have brought forth the Spirit of Thy Salvation, which Thou hast poured forth upon the earth. They that inhabit the earth shall fall, they shall rise that are in the graves. For the dew which is from Thee is health for them but the land of the wicked shall perish. Go, O my people, and enter into thy chambers; hide thyself for a little until the Lord's wrath pass by."

68. How well did he by the chambers point out the tombs of the dead, in which for a brief space we are hidden, that we may be better able to pass to the judgment of God, which shall try us with the indignation due for our wickedness's. He, then, is alive who is hidden and at rest, as though withdrawing himself from our midst and retiring, lest the misery of this world should entangle him with closer snares, for whom the heavenly oracles affirm by the voices of the prophets that the joy of the resurrection is reserved, and the soundness of their freed bodies procured by the divine deed. And dew is well used

as a sign, since by it all vital seeds of the earth are raised to growth. What wonder is it, then, if the dust and ashes also of our failing body grow vigorous by the richness of the heavenly dew, and by the reception of this vital moistening the shapes of our limbs are refashioned and connected again with each other?

69. And the holy prophet Ezekiel teaches and describes with a full exposition how vigor is restored to the dry bones, the senses return, motion is added, and the sinews coming back, the joints of the human body grow strong; how the bones which were very dry are clothed with restored flesh, and the course of the veins and the flow of the blood is covered by the veil of the skin drawn over them. As we read, the reviving multitude of human bodies seems to spring up under the very words of the prophet, and one can see on the widespread plain the new seed shoot forth.

70. But if the wise men of old believed that a crop of armed men sprang up in the district of Thebes from the sowing of the hydra's teeth, whereas it is certainly established that seeds of one kind cannot be changed into another kind of plant, nor bring forth produce differing from its own seeds, so that men should spring from serpents and flesh from teeth; how much more, indeed, is it to be believed that whatever has been sown rises again in its own nature, and that crops do not differ from their seed, that soft things do not spring from hard, nor hard from soft, nor is poison changed into blood; but that flesh is restored from flesh, bone from bone, blood from blood, the humors of the body from humors. Can ye then, ye heathen, who are able to assert a change, deny a

restoration of the nature? Can you refuse to believe the oracles of God, the Gospel, and the prophets, who believe empty fables?

71. But let us now hear the prophet himself, who speaks thus: "The hand of the Lord was upon me, and the Lord led me forth in the Spirit, and placed me in the midst of the plain, and it was full of men's bones; and He led me through them round about, and, lo, there were very many bones on the face of the plain, and they were very dry. And He said unto me: Son of man, can these bones live? And I said: Lord, Thou knows; and He said to me: Prophesy over these bones, and thou shalt say unto them: O ye dry bones, hear the word of the Lord. Thus says the Lord to these bones: Behold I bring upon you the Spirit of life, and I will lay sinews upon you, and will bring up flesh upon you, and will stretch skin over you, and will put My Spirit into you, and ye shall live, and know that I am the Lord. And I prophesied as He commanded me. And it came to pass when I was prophesying all these things, lo, there was a great earthquake."

72. Note how the prophet shows that there was hearing and movement in the bones before the Spirit of life was poured upon them. For, above, both the dry bones are bidden to hear, as if they had the sense of hearing, and that upon this each of them came to its own joint is pointed out by the words of the prophet, for we read as follows: "And the bones came together, each one to its joint. And I beheld, and, lo, sinews and flesh were forming upon them, and skin came upon them from above, and there was no Spirit in them."

73. Great is the lovingkindness of the Lord, that the prophet is taken as a witness of the future resurrection, that we, too might see it with his eyes. For all could not be taken as witnesses, but in that one all we are witnesses, for neither does lying come upon a holy man, nor error upon so great a prophet.

74. Nor ought it to appear at all improbable, that at the command of God the bones were fitted again to their joints, since we have numberless instances in which nature has obeyed the commands of heaven; as the earth was bidden to bring forth the green herb, and did bring it forth; as the rock at the touch of the rod gave forth water for the thirsting people; and the hard stone poured forth streams by the mercy of God for those parched with heat. What else did the rod changed into a serpent signify, than that at the will of God living things can be produced from those that are without life? Do you think it more incredible that bones should come together when bidden, than that streams should be turned back or the sea flee? For thus does the prophet testify: "The sea saw it and fled, Jordan was driven back." Nor can there be any doubt about this fact, which was proved by the rescue of one and the destruction of the other of two peoples, that the waves of the sea stood restrained, and at the same time surrounded one people, and poured back upon the other for their death, that they might overwhelm the one, but preserve the other. And what do we find in the Gospel itself? Did not the Lord Himself prove there that the sea grew calm at a word, the clouds were driven away, the blasts of the winds yielded, and that on the quieted shores the dumb elements obeyed God?

75. But let us go on with the other points, that we may observe how by the Spirit of life the dead are quickened, they that lie in the graves arise, and the tombs are opened: "And He said unto me: Prophesy, son of man, and say to the Spirit, Come from the four winds of heaven, O Spirit, and breathe upon these dead, that they may live. And I prophesied as He commanded me, and the Spirit of life entered into them, and they lived, and stood up on their feet, an exceeding great company. And the Lord spoke unto me, saying: Son of man, these bones are the whole house of Israel. For they say, Our bones are become dry, our hope is lost, we shall perish. Therefore, prophesy and say: Thus says the Lord: Behold I will open your graves, and will bring you up out of your graves into the land of Israel, and ye shall know that I am the Lord, when I shall open your graves, and bring forth My people out of the graves, and shall put My Spirit in you, and place you in your own land, and ye shall know that I am the Lord; I have spoken, and I will perform it, says the Lord."

76. We notice here how the operations of the Spirit of life are again resumed; we know after what manner the dead are raised from the opening tombs. And is it in truth a matter of wonder that the sepulchers of the dead are unclosed at the bidding of the Lord, when the whole earth from its utmost limits is shaken by one thunderclap, the sea overflows its bounds, and again checks the course of its waves? And finally, he who has believed that the dead shall rise again "in a moment, in the twinkling of an eye, at the last trump (for the trumpet shall sound)," "shall be caught up amongst the first in the clouds to meet Christ in the air;" he who has not believed shall be left, and subject himself to the sentence by his own unbelief.

77. The Lord also shows us in the Gospel, to come now to instances, after what manner we shall rise again. "For He raised not Lazarus alone, but the faith of all; and if thou believes, as thou reads, thy spirit also, which was dead, revives with Lazarus." For what does it mean, that the Lord went to the sepulcher and cried with a loud voice, "Lazarus, come forth," except that He would give us a visible proof, would set forth an example of the future resurrection? Why did He cry with a loud voice, as though He were not wont to work in the Spirit, to command in silence, but only that He might show that which is written: "In a moment, in the twinkling of an eye, at the last trump the dead shall rise again incorruptible"? For the raising of the voice answers to the peal of trumpets. And He cried, "Lazarus, come forth." Why is the name added, except perchance lest one might seem to be raised instead of another, or that the resurrection were rather accidental than commanded.

78. So, then, the dead man heard, and came forth from the tomb, bound hand and foot with grave cloths, and his face was bound with a napkin. Conceive, if thou canst, how he makes his way with closed eyes, directs his steps with bound feet, and moves as though free with fastened limbs. The bands remained on him but did not restrain him, his eyes were covered yet they saw. So, then, he saw who was rising again, who was walking, who was leaving the sepulcher. For when the power of the divine command was working, nature did not require its own functions, and brought, as it were, into extremity, obeyed no longer its own course, but the divine will. The bands of death were

burst before those of the grave. The power of moving was exercised before the means of moving were supplied.

79. If thou marvels at this, consider Who gave the command, that thou mayest cease to wonder; Jesus Christ. the Power of God, the Life, the Light, the Resurrection of the dead. The Power raised up him that was lying prostrate, the Life produced his steps, the Light drove away the darkness and restored his sight, the Resurrection renewed the gift of life.

80. Perchance it may trouble thee that the Jews took away the stone and loosened the grave cloths, and thou mayest haply be anxious as to who shall move the stone from thy tomb. As though He Who could restore the Spirit could not remove the stone; or He Who made the bound to walk could not burst the bonds; or He Who had shed light upon the covered eyes could not uncover the face; or He Who could renew the course of nature could not cleave the stone! But, in order that they may believe their eyes who will not believe with their heart, they remove the stone, they see the corpse, they smell the stench, they loose the grave cloths. They cannot deny that he is dead whom they behold rising again; they see the signs of death and the proofs of life. What if, whilst they are busied, they are converted by the very toil itself? What if, while they hear, they believe their own ears? What if, while they behold, they are instructed by their own eyes? What if, while they loose the bonds, they free their own minds? What if, while Lazarus is being unbound, the people is set free, while they let Lazarus go, themselves return to the Lord? For, lastly, many who had come to Mary, seeing what had taken place, believed.

81. And this was not the only instance which our Lord Jesus Christ set forth, but He raised others also, that we might at any rate believe more numerous instances. He raised the young man again, moved by the tears of his widowed mother, when He came and touched the bier, and said: "Young man, I say unto thee, arise, and he that was dead sat up and began to speak." As soon as he heard he forthwith sat up, he forthwith spoke. The working of power, then, is one thing, the order of nature is another.

82. And what shall I say of the daughter of the ruler of the synagogue, at whose death multitudes were weeping and the flute-players piping? For the funeral solemnities were being performed because of the conviction of death. How quickly at the word of the Lord does the spirit return, the reviving body rise up, and food is taken, that the evidence of life may be believed!

83. And why should we wonder that the soul is restored at the word of God, that flesh returns to the bones, when we remember the dead raised by the touch of the prophet's body? Elijah prayed, and raised the dead child. Peter in the name of Christ bade Tabitha rise and walk, and the poor rejoicing believed for the food's sake which she ministered to them, and shall we not believe for our salvation's sake? They purchased the resurrection of another by their tears, shall we not believe in the purchase of ours by the Passion of Christ? Who when He gave up the ghost, in order to show that He died for our resurrection, worked out the course of the resurrection; for so soon as "He cried again with a loud voice and gave up the ghost, the earth did quake, and the rocks were rent, and the tombs were opened, and many bodies of the saints

which slept arose, and, going forth out of the tombs after His resurrection, came into the holy city and appeared unto many."

84. If these things happened when He gave up the ghost, why should we think them incredible when He shall return to judgment? especially since this earlier resurrection is a pledge of that future resurrection, and a pattern of that reality Which is to come; indeed, it is rather itself truth than a pattern. Who, then, at the Lord's resurrection opened the graves, gave a hand to those who were rising, showed them the road to find the holy city? If there was no one, it was certainly the Divine Power which was working in the bodies of the dead. Shall one seek for the aid of man where one sees the work of God?

85. Divine action has no need of human assistance. God commanded that the heavens should come into existence, and it was done; He determined that the earth should be created, and it was created. Who carried together the stones on his shoulders? who supplied the expenses? who furnished assistance to God as He toiled? These things were made in a moment. Would you know how quickly? "He spoke and they were made." If the elements spring up at a word, why should the dead not rise at a word? For though they be dead, yet they once lived, once had the breath of life for feeling, and strength for acting; and there is a very great difference between not having been
capable of life, and having remained lifeless. The devil said: "Command this stone that it become bread." He confesses that at the command of God nature can be transformed, dost thou not believe that at the command of God nature can be remade?

86. Philosophers dispute about the course of the sun and the system of the heavens, and there are those who think that these should be believed when they are ignorant of what they are talking about. For neither have they climbed up into the heavens, nor measured the sky, nor examined the universe with their eyes; for none of them was with God in the beginning, none of them has said of God: "When He was preparing the heavens I was with Him, I was with Him as a master workman, I was he in whom He delighted." If, then, they are believed, is God not believed, Who says: "As the new heavens and the new earth, which I make to remain before Me, says the Lord; so shall your name and your seed abide; and month shall be after month, and Sabbath after Sabbath, and all flesh shall come in My sight to worship in Jerusalem, says the Lord God; and they shall go forth, and shall see the limbs of men who have transgressed against Me. For their worm shall not die and their fire shall not be quenched and they shall be a sight to all flesh."

87. If the earth and heaven are renewed, why should we doubt that man, on account of whom heaven and earth were made, can be renewed? If the transgressor be reserved for punishment, why should not the just be kept for glory? If the worm of sins does not die, how shall the flesh of the just perish? For the resurrection, as the very form of the word shows, is this, that what has fallen should rise again, that which has died should come to life again.

88. And this is the course and ground of justice, that since the action of body and soul is common to both (for what

the soul has conceived the body has carried out), each should come into judgment, and each should be either given over to punishment or reserved for glory. For it would seem almost inconsistent that, since the law of the mind fights against the law of the flesh, and the mind often, when sin dwelling in man acts, does that which it hates; the mind guilty of a fault shared by another should be subjected to penalty, and the flesh, the author of the evil, should enjoy rest: and that should alone suffer which had not sinned alone, or should alone attain to glory, not having fought alone with the help of grace.

89. The reason, unless I am mistaken, is complete and just, but I do not require a reason from Christ. If I am convinced by reason I reject faith. Abraham believed God, let us also believe Him, that we who are heirs of his race may also be heirs of his faith. David likewise believed, and therefore did he speak; let us also believe that we may be able to speak, knowing that "He Who raised up the Lord Jesus shall raise up us also with Jesus." For God, Who never lies, promised this; the Truth promised this in His Gospel, when He said: "This is the will of Him that sent Me, that of all that which He hath given Me I should lose nothing, but should raise it up at the last day." And He thought it not sufficient to have said this once, but marked it by express repetition, for this follows: "For this is the will of My Father, Who sent Me, that every one that sees the Son and believeth on Him should have eternal life, and I will raise him up at the last day."

90. Who was He that said this? He in truth Who when dead raised up many bodies of the departed. If we believe not God, shall we not believe evidence? Do we not

believe what He promised, since He did even that which He did not promise? And what reason would He have had for dying, had He not also had a reason for rising again? For, seeing that God could not die, Wisdom could not die; and inasmuch as that could not rise again which had not died, flesh is assumed, which can die, that whilst that, whose nature it is, dies, that which had died should rise again. For the resurrection could not be effected except by man; since, "as by man came death, so too by man came the resurrection of the dead."

91. So, then, man rose because man died; man was raised again, but God raised him. Then it was man according to the Flesh, now God is all in all. For now we know not Christ according to the flesh, but we possess the grace of that Flesh, so that we know Him the first fruits of them that rest, the firstborn of the dead. Now the first-fruits are undoubtedly of the same nature and kind as the remaining fruits, the first of which are offered to God as a petition for a richer increase, as a holy thank-offering for all gifts, and as a kind of libation of that nature which has been restored. Christ, then, is the first fruits of them that rest. But is this of His own who are at rest, who, as it were, freed from death, are holden by a kind of sweet slumber, or of all those who are dead? "As in Christ all die, so too in Christ shall all be made alive." So, then, as the first fruits of death were in Adam, so also the first fruits of the resurrection are in Christ.

92. All men rise again, but let no one lose heart, and let not the just grieve at the common lot of rising again, since he awaits the chief fruit of his virtue. All indeed shall rise again, but, as says the Apostle, "each in his own order."

The fruit of the Divine Mercy is common to all, but the order of merit differs. The day gives light to all, the sun warms all, the rain fertilizes the possessions of all with genial showers.

93. We are all born, and we shall all rise again, but in each state, whether of living or of living again, grace differs and the condition differs. For, "in a moment, in the twinkling of an eye, at the last trump, the dead shall rise incorruptible and we shall be changed." Moreover, in death itself some rest, and some live. Rest is good, but life is better. And so the Apostle rouses him that is resting to life, saying: "Rise, thou that sleeps, and arise from the dead, and Christ shall give thee light." Therefore he is aroused that he may live, that he may be like to Paul, that he may be able to say: "For we that are alive shall not prevent those that are asleep." He speaks not here of the common manner of life, and the breath which we all alike enjoy, but of the merit of the resurrection. For, having said, "And the dead which are in Christ shall rise first," he adds further; "And we that are alive shall together with them be caught up in the clouds, to meet Christ in the air."

94. Paul certainly is dead, and by his honorable passion exchanged the life of the body for everlasting glory; did he then deceive himself when he wrote that he should be caught up alive in the clouds to meet Christ? We read the same too of Enoch and of Elijah, and thou too shalt be caught up in the Spirit. Lo the chariot of Elijah, lo the fire, though not seen are prepared, that the just may ascend, the innocent be borne forth, and thy life may not know death. For indeed the apostles knew not death, according to that which was said: "Verily, verily, I say unto you, many of

those standing here shall not taste death until they see the Son of man coming in His kingdom." For he lives, who has nothing in him which can die, who has not from Egypt any shoe or bond, but has put it off before laying aside the service of this body. And so not Enoch alone is alive, for not he alone was caught up; Paul also was caught up to meet Christ.

95. The patriarchs also live, for God could not be called the God of Abraham, of Isaac, and of Jacob, except the dead were living; for He is not the God of the dead but of the living. And we, too, shall live if we be willing to copy the deeds and habits of our predecessors. We are astonished at the rewards of the patriarchs, let us copy their faithfulness; we tell of their grace, let us follow
their obedience; let us not, enticed by appetite, fall into the snares of the world. Let us lay hold of the opportunity, of the commandment of the Law, the mercy of our vocation, the desire of suffering. The patriarchs went forth from their own land, let us go forth in purpose from the power of the body; let us go forth in purpose as they in exile; but they esteemed that not to be exile which the
fear of God caused, necessity did not enforce. They changed their land for another soil, let us change earth for heaven; they changed in earthly habitation, let us change in spirit. To them Wisdom showed the heaven illuminated with stars, let it enlighten the eyes of our heart. Thus does the type agree with the truth, and the truth with the type.

96. Abraham, ready to receive strangers, faithful towards God, devoted in ministering, quick in his service, saw the Trinity in a type; he added religious duty to hospitality, when beholding Three he worshipped One, and

preserving the distinction of the Persons, yet addressed one Lord, he offered to Three the honor of his gift, while acknowledging one Power. It was not learning but grace which spoke in him, and he believed better what he had not learnt than we who have learnt. No one had falsified the representation of the truth, and so he sees Three, but worships the Unity. He brings forth three measures of fine meal, and slays one victim, considering that one sacrifice is sufficient, but a triple gift; one victim, an offering of three. And in the four kings, who does not understand that he subjected to himself the elements of the material creation, and all earthly things in a sign whereby the Lord's Passion was prefigured? Faithful in war, moderate in his triumph, in that he preferred not to become richer by the gifts of men, but by those of God.

97. He believed that he when old could beget a son, and judged himself when a father able to sacrifice his son; nor did his fatherly affection tremble when duty aided the right hand of the old man, for he knew that his son would be more acceptable to God when sacrificed than when whole. Therefore he brings his well-beloved son to be sacrificed, and offered promptly him whom he had received late; nor is he restrained by being called by the name of father, when his son called him "Father," and he replied, "My son." Dear pledges of love are these names, but the commands of God are loved still more. And so although their hearts felt for each other, their purpose remained firm. The father's hand stretched out the knife over his son, and the father's heart struck the blow that the sentence might not fail of being carried out; he feared lest the stroke should miss, lest his right hand should fail. He felt the moving of fatherly affection, but did not shrink

from the work of submission, and hastened his obedience, even when he heard the voice from heaven. Let us then set God before all those whom we love, father, brother, mother, that He may preserve for us those whom we love, as in the case of Abraham we behold rather the liberal Rewarder than the servant.

98. The father offered indeed his son, but God is appeased not by blood but by dutiful obedience. He showed the ram in the thicket in the stead of the lad, that He might restore the son to his father, and yet the victim not fail the priest. And so Abraham was not stained with his son's blood, nor was God deprived of the sacrifice. The prophet spoke, and neither yielded to boastfulness nor continued obstinate, but took the ram in exchange for the lad. And by this is shown the more how piously he offered him whom he now so gladly received back. And thou, if thou offer thy gift to God, dost not lose it. But we are tenacious of our own; God gave His only Son for us, we refuse ours. Abraham saw this and recognized the mystery, that salvation should be to us from the Tree, nor did it escape his notice that in one and the same sacrifice it was One that seemed to be offered, Another which could be slain.

99. Let us, then, imitate the devotion of Abraham, let us imitate the goodness of Isaac, let us imitate his purity. The man was plainly good and chaste, full of devotion towards God, chaste towards his wife. He returned not evil for evil, yielded to those who would thrust him out, received them again on their repentance, neither violent towards insolence, nor stubborn towards kindness. Fleeing from strife when he went away from others, ready to forgive when he received them again, and still more lavish of

goodness when he forgave them. The fellowship of his company was sought, he gave in addition a feast of pleasure.

100. In Jacob, too, let us imitate the type of Christ, let there be some likeness of his actions in ourselves. We shall have our share with him, if we imitate him. He was obedient to his mother, he yielded to his brother, he served his father-in-law, he sought his wages from the increase, not from a division of the flocks. There was no covetous division, where his portion brought such gain. Nor was that sign without a purpose, the ladder from earth to heaven, wherein was seen the future fellowship between men and angels through the cross of Christ, whose thigh was paralyzed, that in his thigh he might recognize the Heir of his body, and foretell by the paralyzing of his thigh the Passion of his Heir.

101. We see, then, that heaven is open to virtue, and that this is the privilege not only of a few: "For many shall come from the east and from the west, and the north and the south, and shall sit down in the kingdom of God," giving expression to the enjoyment of perpetual rest since the motions of their souls are stilled. Let us follow Abraham in our habits, that he may receive us into his bosom, and cherish us with loving embrace, like Lazarus the inheritor of his humility surrounded by his own special virtues. The followers of the holy patriarch, approved of God, cherish us not in a bodily bosom, but in a clothing as it were of good works. "Be not deceived," says the Apostle, "God is not mocked."

102. We have seen, then, how grave an offence it is not to believe the resurrection; for if we rise not again, then

Christ died in vain, then Christ rose not again. For if He rose not for us, He certainly rose not at all, for He had no need to rise for Himself. The universe rose again in Him, the heaven rose again in Him, the earth rose again in Him, for there shall be a new heaven and a new earth. But where was the necessity of a resurrection for Him Whom the claims of death held not? For though He died as man, yet was He free in hell itself.

103. Wilt thou know how free? "I am become as a man that hath no help, free among the dead." And well is He called free, Who had power to raise Himself, according to that which is written: "Destroy this temple, and in three days I will raise it up." And well is He called free, Who had descended to rescue others. For He was made as a man, not, indeed, in appearance only, but so fashioned in truth, for He is man, and who shall know Him? For, "being made in the likeness of men, and being found in fashion as a man, He humbled Himself, becoming obedient even unto death," in order that through that obedience we might see His glory, "the glory as of the Only-begotten of the Father," according to Saint John. For thus is the statement of Scripture preserved, if both the glory of the Only-begotten and the nature of perfect man are preserved in Christ.

104. And so He needed no helper. For He needed none when He made the world, so as to need none when He would redeem it. No legate, no messenger, but the Lord Himself made it whole. "He spoke and it was done." The Lord Himself made it whole, Himself in every part, because all things were by Him. For who should help Him in Whom all things were created and by Whom all things

consist? Who should help Him Who makes all things in a moment, and raises the dead at the last trump? The "last," not as though He could not raise them at the first, or the second, or the third, but an order is observed, not that a difficulty may be at last overcome, but that the prescribed number be accomplished.

105. But it is now time, I think, to speak of the trumpets since my discourse is nearing its end, that the trumpet may also be the sign of the finishing of my address. We read of seven trumpets in the Revelation of John, which seven angels received. And there you read that when the seventh angel sounded his trumpet, there was a great voice from heaven, saying: "The kingdom of this world is become the kingdom of our God and of His Christ, and He shall reign for ever and ever." The word trumpet is also used for a voice, as you read: "Behold a door opened in heaven, and the first voice which I heard, as of a trumpet speaking with me and saying, Come up hither, and I will show thee the things which must come to pass." We read also: "Blow up the trumpet at the beginning of the month [the new moon]"; and again elsewhere: "Praise Him with the sound of the trumpet."

106. Therefore we ought with all our power to observe what is the signification of the trumpets, lest, accepting them, like old women, as part of the story, we should be in danger if we were to think things unworthy of spiritual teaching, or not befitting the dignity of the Scriptures. For when we read that our warfare is not against flesh and blood, but against spiritual hosts of wickedness, which are in high places, we ought not to think of weapons of the flesh, but of such as are mighty before God. It is not

enough that one see the trumpet or hear its sound, unless one understands the signification of the sound. For if the trumpet give an uncertain sound, how shall one prepare himself for war? Wherefore it is important that we understand the meaning of the voice of the trumpet, lest we seem barbarians, when we either hear or utter trumpet-sounds of this sort. And therefore when we speak, let us pray that the Holy Spirit would interpret them to us.

107. Let us, then, investigate what we read in the Old Testament concerning the kinds of trumpets, considering that those festivals which were enjoined on the Jews by the Law are the shadow of joys above and of heavenly festivals. For here is the shadow, there the truth. Let us endeavor to attain to the truth by means of the shadow. Of which truth the figure is expressed in this manner, where we read that the Lord said to Moses: "Speak unto the children of Israel, saying, In the seventh month, on the first day of the month, shall be a rest unto you, a memorial of blowing of trumpets, it shall be called holy unto you. Ye shall not do any servile work, and ye shall kindle a whole burnt-offering unto the Lord." And in the Book of Numbers: "The Lord spoke unto Moses, saying: Make thee two trumpets of beaten work, of silver shalt thou make them, and they shall be to thee for calling the assembly and for the journeying of the camp. And thou shalt blow with them, and all the congregation shall be gathered together at the door of the tabernacle of witness. But if thou blow with one trumpet, all the princes and leaders of Israel shall come to thee; and ye shall blow a signal with the trumpet the first time, and they shall move the camp forward, and place it on the east. And ye shall blow a signal with the trumpet the second time, and they

shall move the camp forward, and place it towards Libanus. And ye shall blow a signal with the trumpet the third time, and they shall move the camp forward, which shall be placed towards the north [Boream]. And ye shall blow a signal with the trumpet the fourth time, and they shall move the camp forward, which shall be placed towards the north [Aquilonem]. They shall blow a signal with the trumpet when they move forward. And when ye shall gather together the assembly, blow with the trumpet, but not the signal. And the sons of Aaron, the priests, shall blow with the trumpets, and it shall be for you a statute for ever throughout your generations. But if ye shall go out to war into your own land, against the adversaries who resist you, ye shall sound a signal with the trumpets and ye shall be remembered before the Lord, and have deliverance from your dead. Also in the days of your gladness, and on your feast days, and on your new moons, ye shall blow with the trumpets, and at your whole burnt sacrifices and at your peace-offerings, and it shall be for you for your memorial before the Lord, says the Lord."

108. What then? shall we esteem festival days by eating and drinking? But let no man judge us in respect of eating; "for we know that the Law is spiritual. Let no man therefore judge us in any meats or in drink, or in respect of a feast day or new moons, or a Sabbath day, which are a shadow of the things to come, but the body is of Christ." Let us, then, seek the body of Christ which the voice of the Father, from heaven, as it were the last trumpet, has shown to you at the time when the Jews said that it thundered; the body of Christ, which again the last trump shall reveal; for "the Lord Himself shall descend from

heaven at the voice of the Archangel, and at the trump of God, and they that are dead in Christ shall rise again;" for "where the body is, there too are the eagles," where the body of Christ is, there is the truth.

108. The seventh trumpet, then, seems to signify the Sabbath of the week, which is reckoned not only in days and years and periods (for which reason the number of the jubilee is sacred), but includes also the seventieth year, when the people returned to Jerusalem, who had remained seventy years in captivity. In hundreds also and in thousands the observation of the sacred number is by no means passed over, for not without a meaning did the Lord say: "I have left the seven thousand men, who have not bent their knees before Baal." Therefore the shadow of the future rest is figured in time in the days, months, and years of this world, and therefore the children of Israel are commanded by Moses, that in the seventh month, on the first day of the month, a rest should be established for all at the "memorial of the trumpets;" and that no servile work should be done, but a sacrifice be offered to God, because that at the end of the week, as it were the Sabbath of the world, spiritual and not bodily work is required of us. For that which is bodily is servile, for the body serves the soul, but innocence makes free, guilt reduces to slavery.

109. It was necessary, then, that spiritual things should be made known as in a mirror and in a riddle; "For now we see by means of a mirror, but then face to face." Now we war after the flesh, then in the Spirit we shall see the divine mysteries. Let, then, the character of the true law be expressed in our manner of life, who walk in the image

of God, for the shadow of the Law has now passed away. The carnal Jews had the shadow, the likeness is ours, the reality theirs who shall rise again. For we know that according to the Law there are these three, the shadow, the image or likeness, and the reality; the shadow in the Law, the image in the Gospel, the truth in the judgment.

But all is Christ's, and all is in Christ, Whom now we cannot see according to the reality, but we see Him, as it were, in a kind of likeness of future things, of which we have seen the shadow in the Law. So, then, Christ is not the shadow but the likeness of God, not an empty likeness but the reality. And so the Law was by Moses, for the shadow was through man, the likeness was through the Law, the reality through Jesus. For reality cannot proceed from any other source than from reality.

110. If, then, any one desires to see this Image of God, he must love God, that he may be loved by God; and be no longer a servant but a friend, because he has kept the commandments of God, that he may enter into the cloud where God is. Let him make to himself two reasonable trumpets of beaten work of proved silver, that is, composed of precious words and adorned, from which not a harsh shrill sound with dread-inspiring voice may be uttered, but high thanks to God may be poured forth with continuous exultation. For by the voice of such trumpets the dead are raised, not indeed by the sound of the metal, but aroused by the word of truth. And perchance it is those two trumpets by which Paul, through the Divine Spirit, spoke when he said: "I will pray with the Spirit, and I will pray with the understanding, I will sing with the Spirit, and I will sing with the understanding;" for the one

without the other seems by no means to have perfect utterance.

111. Yet it is not every one's business to sound each trumpet, nor every one's business to call together the whole assembly, but that prerogative is granted to the priests alone, and the ministers of God who sound the trumpets, so that whosoever shall hear and follow thither where the glory of the Lord is, and shall with early determination come to the tabernacle of witness, may be able also to see the divine works, and merit that appointed and eternal home for the entire succession of his posterity. For then is the war finished and the enemy put to flight, when the grace of the Spirit and the energy of the soul act together.

112. And these are salutary trumpets also, if one believe with the heart, and confess with the mouth; "For with the heart man believeth unto righteousness, and with the mouth confession is made unto salvation." For with this twofold trumpet man arrives at that holy land, namely, the grace of the resurrection. Let them, then, ever sound to thee, that thou mayest ever hear the voice of God; may the utterances of the Angels and Prophets ever incite and move thee, that thou mayest hasten to things above.

113. David was thinking of this purpose in his breast when he said: "For I will pass into the place of the marvelous tabernacle, even to the house of God, with the voice of exultation and thanksgiving, the sound of one that feasts." For not only are enemies overcome by the sound of these trumpets; but without them there could not be rejoicings, and festivals or new moons. For no one,

unless he have received the promises of the Divine Word, and believes the message derived therefrom, can keep festivals or new moons, in which he desires to fill himself, freed from bodily pleasure and secular occupation, with the light of Christ. And sacrifices themselves cannot be pleasing to Christ unless confession of the mouth accompanies them, which according to custom stirs up the people to implore the grace of God at the priestly oblation.

114. Let us therefore be preachers of the Lord, and praise Him in the sound of the trumpet, not thinking little or lightly of its power, but such things as can fill the ear of the mind, and enter into the depths of our inmost consciousness, so that we think not that what suits to the body is to be applied to the Godhead, nor measure the greatness of Divine Power by human might, so as to
enquire how any one can rise again, or with what kind of body he will come, or how that which has been dissolved can again coalesce, and what is lost be restored, for all these things are accomplished as soon as they are determined by the Divine Will. And it is not a sound of a trumpet distinguishable by the bodily senses which is expected, but the invisible power of the Majesty of heaven operates; for with God to will is to do; nor need we enquire into the force required for the resurrection, but seek its fruit for ourselves. Which will be accomplished all the more easily, if freed from faults we attain to the fullness of the spiritual mystery, and the renewed flesh receives grace from the Spirit, and the soul obtains from Christ the brightness of eternal light.

115. But those mysteries pertain not to individuals only, but to the whole human race. For observe the order of grace according to the type of the Law. When the first trumpet sounds, it collects those towards the east, as the chief and elect; when the second sounds, those nearly equal in merit, who, being placed towards Libanus, have abandoned the follies of the nations; when the third, those who as it were, tossed on the sea of this world, have been driven hither and thither by the waves of this life; when the fourth, those who have by no means been able sufficiently to soften the hardness of their hearts by the commandments of spiritual utterance, and therefore are said to be towards the north—for, according to Solomon, the north is a hard wind.

116. And so although all are raised again in a moment, yet all are raised in the order of their merits. And therefore they rise first, who yielding early to the impulses of devotion, and as it were going forth before the rising dawn of faith, received the rays of the eternal Sun. This one may rightly say either of the patriarchs in the course of the Old Testament, or of the apostles under the Gospel. And the second are they who, forsaking the rites of the Gentiles, passed from unholy error under the training of the Church. So, then, those first were of the fathers, those second of the Gentiles, for the light of faith took its beginning from those, among these it will remain to the end of the world. In the third place and in the fourth, those are raised who are in the south and in the north. The earth is divided into these four, of these four is the year made up, in these four is the earth completed, and from these four is the Church collected. For all who are considered to be joined to holy Church, by being called by the Divine Name, shall obtain the privilege of the resurrection and

the grace of eternal bliss, for "they shall come from the east and west, and from the north and south, and shall sit down in the kingdom of God."

117. For it is no small light wherewith Christ encompasses His world: since "His going forth is from the height of heaven, and His progress to the height thereof, nor is there any who can hide himself from His heat." For with His Goodness He enlightens all, and wills not to reject but to amend the foolish, and desires not to exclude the hard-hearted from the Church, but to soften them. And so the Church in the Song of Songs and Christ in the Gospel invites them, saying: "Come unto Me, all ye who labor and are heavy laden, and I will refresh you; take My yoke upon you and learn of Me, for I am meek and lowly in heart."

118. And you may recognize also the voice of the invitation of the Church, for she says: "Awake, O north wind, and come, thou south, blow upon my garden, and let my ointment flow forth. Let my brother come down into his garden and eat the fruit of his precious trees." For knowing even then, O holy Church, that from those also there would be fruitful works for thee, thou didst promise to thy Christ fruit from such as they, thou who didst first say that thou was brought into the King's chamber, loving His breast above wine, since thou loves Him Who loved thee, sought Him Who fed thee, and didst despise dangers for religion's sake.

119. And then, O Bride, thou art called to come from Libanus, being in the Lord's judgment all fair and without fault. For thus it is written: "Thou art all fair, my love,

and there is no fault in thee. Come hither from Libanus, my bride, come hither from Libanus."

120. Afterwards, thou, fearing no rushing waters, no torrents coming down from Libanus, calls the north and south winds, wishing them to blow upon thy garden, that thy ointment may flow forth upon others, and that thou mayest offer to Christ in others the manifold fruits of thy productiveness.

121. And therefore "blessed is he who keeps the words of this prophecy," which has revealed the resurrection to us by clearer testimony, saying: "And I saw the dead, great and small, standing before the throne, and they opened the books; and another book was opened, which is the book of life; and the dead were judged out of the things which were written in the books, according to their works. And the sea gave up the dead which were in it, and hell gave up the dead which were in it." We must, then, not question how they shall rise again, whom hell gives up and the sea restores.

122. Hear also when the future grace of the just is promised: "And I heard," he says, "a great voice from the throne saying: Behold, the tabernacle of God is with men, and He shall dwell with them, and they shall be His people, and God Himself shall be their God with them: and He shall wipe away every tear from their eyes; and death shall be no more, nor mourning, nor crying, nor pain, any more."

123. Compare now, if you will, and contrast this life with that; and choose, if you then can, unending bodily existence in toil, and in the wretched misery of such

changes as we endure, in satiety when we have our wishes, in that disgust which attends our pleasures. If God were willing to let these last for ever, would you choose them? For if on its own account life is to be escaped from, that there may be an avoidance of troubles and rest from miseries, how much more is that rest to be sought for, which shall be followed by the eternal pleasure of the resurrection to come, where there is no succession of faults, no enticement to sin?

124. Who is so patient in suffering as not to pray for death? who has such endurance in weakness as not to wish rather to die than to live in debility? Who is so brave in sorrow as not to desire to escape from it even by death? But if we ourselves are dissatisfied while life lasts, although we know that a limit is fixed for it, how much more weary should we become of this life if we saw that the troubles of the body would be with us without end! For who is there who would wish to be excepted from death? Or what would be more unendurable than a miserable immortality? "If in this life only," he says, "we hope in Christ, we are more miserable than all men;" not because to hope in Christ is miserable, but because Christ has prepared another life for those who hope in Him. For this life is liable to sin, that life is reserved for the reward.

125. And how much weariness do we find that the short stages of our lives bring us! The boy longs to be a young man; the youth counts the years leading to riper age; the young man, unthankful for the advantage of his vigorous time of life, desires the honor of old age. And so to all there comes naturally the desire of change, because we are dissatisfied with that which we now are. And lastly,

even the things we have desired are wearisome to us; and what we have wished to obtain, when we have obtained it, we dislike.

126. Wherefore holy men have not without reason often lamented their lengthy dwelling here: David lamented it, Jeremiah lamented it, and Elijah lamented it. If we believe wise men, and those in whom the Divine Spirit dwelt, they were hastening to better things; and if we enquire as to the judgment of others, that we may ascertain that all agree in one opinion, what great men have preferred death to sorrow, what great men have preferred it to fear! esteeming forsooth the fear of death to be worse than death itself. So death is not feared on account of evils which belong to it, but is preferred to the miseries of life, since the departure of the dying is desired and the dread of the living is avoided.

127. So be it, then. Granted that the Resurrection is preferable to this life. What! Have philosophers themselves found anything with which we should have a greater delight to continue than to rise again? Even those indeed who say that souls are immortal do not satisfy me, seeing they only allow me a partial redemption. What grace can that be by which I am not wholly benefited?
What life is that if the operation of God dies out in me? What righteousness is that which, if death is the end of natural existence, is common to the sinner and the just? What is that truth, that the soul should be considered immortal, because it moves itself and is always in motion? As regards that which in the body is common to us with beasts, it is perhaps uncertain what happens

before the body exists, and the truth is not to be gathered from these differences but destroyed.

128. But is their opinion preferable, who say that our souls, when they have passed out of these bodies, migrate into the bodies of beasts, or of various other living creatures? Philosophers, indeed, themselves are wont to argue that these are ridiculous fancies of poets, such as might be produced by draughts of the drugs of Circe; and they say that not so much they who are represented to have undergone such things, as the senses of those who have invented such tales are changed into the forms of various beasts as it were by Circe's cup. For what is so like a marvel as to believe that men could have been changed into the forms of beasts? How much greater a marvel, however, would it be that the soul which rules man should take on itself the nature of a beast so opposed to that of man, and being capable of reason should be able to pass over to an irrational animal, than that the form of the body should have been changed? You yourselves, who teach these things, destroy what you teach. For you have given up the production of these portentous conversions by means of magic incantations.

129. Poets say these things in sport, and philosophers blame them and at the same time they imagine that those very things are true of the dead which they consider fictitious as regards the living. For they who invented such tales did not intend to assert the truth of their own fable, but to deride the errors of philosophers, who think that that same soul which was accustomed to overcome anger by gentle and lowly purpose, can now, inflamed by the raging impulses of a lion, impatient with anger and

with unbridled rage, thirst for blood and seek for slaughter. Or again, that that soul, which as it were by royal counsel used to moderate the various storms of the people, and to calm them with the voice of reason, can now endure to howl in pathless and desert places after the fashion of a wolf; or that that soul which, groaning under a heavy burden, used to low in sad complaint over the labors of the plough, now changed into the fashion of a man, seeks for horns on his smooth brow; or that another, which used of old to be borne aloft on rapid wing to the heights of heaven, now thinks of flight no longer in its power, and mourns that it grows sluggish in the weight of a human body.

130. Perchance you destroyed Icarus through some such teaching, because the youth, led on by your persuasion, imagined, it may be, that he had been a bird. By such means too have many old men been deceived so as to submit to grievous pain, having unhappily believed the fables about swans, and thought that they, whilst soothing their pain with mournful strains, would be able to transmute their gray hair into downy feathers.

131. How incredible are these things! how odious! How much more fitting is it to believe in accordance with nature, in accordance with what takes place in every kind of fruit; to believe in accordance with the pattern of what has happened, in accordance with the utterances of prophets, and the heavenly promise of Christ! For what is better than to be sure that the work of God does not perish, and that those who are made in the image and likeness of God cannot be transformed into the shapes of beasts; since in truth it is not the form of the body but of

the spirit which is made after the likeness of God. For in what manner could man, to whom are subjected the other kinds of living creatures, migrate with the better part of himself into an animal subjected to himself? Nature does not suffer this, and if nature did grace would not.

132. But I have seen what you, Gentiles, think of each other, and indeed it ought not to seem strange that you who worship beasts should believe that you can be changed into beasts. But I had rather that you judged better concerning what is due to you, that you may believe that you will be not in the company of wild beasts, but in the companionship of angels.

133. The soul has to depart from the surroundings of this life, and the pollutions of the earthly body, and to press on to those heavenly companies, though it is for the saints alone, to attain to them, and to sing praise to God (as in the prophet's words we hear of those who are harping and saying: "For great are Thy marvelous works, O Lord God Almighty, just and true are Thy ways, Thou King of the nations; who shall not fear and magnify Thy Name, for Thou only art holy, for all nations shall come and worship before Thee"), and to see Thy marriage feast, O Lord Jesus, in which the Bride is led from earthly to heavenly things, while all rejoice in harmony, for "to Thee shall all flesh come," now no longer subject to transitory things, but joined to the Spirit, to see the chambers adorned with linen, roses, lilies, and garlands. Of whom else is the marriage so adorned? For it is adorned with the purple stripes of confessors, the blood of martyrs, the lilies of virgins, and the crowns of priests.

134. Holy David desired beyond all else for himself that he might behold and gaze upon this, for he says: "One thing have I asked of the Lord, that will I seek after; that I may dwell in the house of the Lord all the days of my life, and see the pleasure of the Lord."

135. It is a pleasure to believe this, a joy to hope for it; and certainly, not to have believed it is a pain, to have lived in this hope a grace. But if I am mistaken in this, that I prefer to be associated after death with angels rather than with beasts, I am gladly mistaken, and so long as I live will never suffer myself to be cheated of this hope.

136. For what comfort have I left but that I hope to come quickly to thee, my brother, and that thy departure will not cause a long severance between us, and that it may be granted me, through thy intercessions, that thou mayest quickly call me who long for thee. For who is there who ought not to wish for himself beyond all else that "this corruptible should put on incorruption, and this mortal put on immortality"? that we who succumb to death through the frailty of the body, being raised above nature, may no longer have to fear death.

www.ingramcontent.com/pod-product-compliance
Lightning Source LLC
Chambersburg PA
CBHW052104070526
44584CB00017B/2331